The Robin Hood Caper

A Comedy in Three Acts

by Fred Carmichael

A Samuel French Acting Edition

New York Hollywood London Toronto
SAMUELFRENCH.COM

Copyright © 1991 by Fred Carmichael

ALL RIGHTS RESERVED

CAUTION: Professionals and amateurs are hereby warned that *THE ROBIN HOOD CAPER* is subject to a Licensing Fee. It is fully protected under the copyright laws of the United States of America, the British Commonwealth, including Canada, and all other countries of the Copyright Union. All rights, including professional, amateur, motion picture, recitation, lecturing, public reading, radio broadcasting, television and the rights of translation into foreign languages are strictly reserved. In its present form the play is dedicated to the reading public only.

The amateur live stage performance rights to *THE ROBIN HOOD CAPER* are controlled exclusively by Samuel French, Inc., and licensing arrangements and performance licenses must be secured well in advance of presentation. PLEASE NOTE that amateur Licensing Fees are set upon application in accordance with your producing circumstances. When applying for a licensing quotation and a performance license please give us the number of performances intended, dates of production, your seating capacity and admission fee. Licensing Fees are payable one week before the opening performance of the play to Samuel French, Inc., at 45 W. 25th Street, New York, NY 10010.

Licensing Fee of the required amount must be paid whether the play is presented for charity or gain and whether or not admission is charged.

Stock licensing fees quoted upon application to Samuel French, Inc.

For all other rights than those stipulated above, apply to: Samuel French, Inc.

Particular emphasis is laid on the question of amateur or professional readings, permission and terms for which must be secured in writing from Samuel French, Inc.

Copying from this book in whole or in part is strictly forbidden by law, and the right of performance is not transferable.

Whenever the play is produced the following notice must appear on all programs, printing and advertising for the play: "Produced by special arrangement with Samuel French, Inc."

Due authorship credit must be given on all programs, printing and advertising for the play.

No one shall commit or authorize any act or omission by which the copyright of, or the right to copyright, this play may be impaired.
No one shall make any changes in this play for the purpose of production.
Publication of this play does not imply availability for performance. Both amateurs and professionals considering a production are strongly advised in their own interests to apply to Samuel French, Inc., for written permission before starting rehearsals, advertising, or booking a theatre.
No part of this book may be reproduced, stored in a retrieval system, or transmitted in any form, by any means, now known or yet to be invented, including mechanical, electronic, photocopying, recording, videotaping, or otherwise, without the prior written permission of the publisher.

ISBN 978-0-573-61484-2   Printed in U.S.A.   #924

STORY OF THE PLAY

"Fred Carmichael has again proved himself an inventive and amusing playwright. He has taken an old, old plot—rob from the rich and give to the poor—but not even Robin Hood would recognize the amusing modern slant given to it," said the reviews when this play opened in summer stock. Starting out as a light comedy, The Robin Hood Caper rises to a pitch of irresistible farce. Four extremely old people meet semi-annually to report on their good works in their "Charities Anonymous Club." This year it is held at the home of Flora Langley's nephew, a small-town journalist in danger of losing his newspaper to the grafting Mayor. It turns out that Flora and her three old friends are actually retired crooks who use their old "modus operandi" for charitable purposes. Through the plot there is woven an unusual love story, clever moments of satire, and show-stopping situations of hilarity. Three of the men's parts and one woman's part are small, the others larger. To quote the press: "The proof of a comedy is in the audience's laughter and this is packed with it." "Where other playwrights strike for the heart, Carmichael strikes the funnybone. He makes plays as other men make model trains, using the theatre as a giant erector set . . . horseplay unlimited with generous helpings of satire."

(Copy of the program of the first performance of THE ROBIN HOOD CAPER as presented in summer stock by the Caravan Theatre at the Dorset Playhouse, Dorset, Vermont, on October 11, 1962.)

THE ROBIN HOOD CAPER

By Fred Carmichael

Staged by the Author

CAST
(In Order of Appearance)

RICHARD COLLINS	*Barry Dunleavey*
FLORA LANGLEY	*Patricia Wyn Rose*
JESSICA SELBY	*Lynnette Mettey*
EMILY JORDAN	*Elizabeth Franz*
JASON BOSLEY	*Charles Miller*
PHILIP MULLINS	*Herman Petras*
HUBERT RATNER	*Fred Carmichael*
WARRFN COATES	*Alvah Bennett*
FREDERICK RUGGLES	*Robert R. Law*
SYLVIA COATES	*Susan Richardson*

The entire action of the play takes place in Richard Collins' house in Bridgeway Corners, Wisconsin. The time is the present.

ACT ONE
Late morning.

ACT TWO
That evening.

ACT THREE
The following morning.

Setting Designed by Judith Page Murray.

The author wishes to thank Judith Page Murray for her cooperation in making this and many other shows possible.

DESCRIPTION OF CHARACTERS

FLORA LANGLEY: She is a very old and very kindly soul. Her manner and spirit are dripping with the milk of human kindness and there is an odd twinkle in her eye as she talks of her desire to help others. She dresses in good clothes although somehow they aren't quite as fashionable as they might be. Being old, she moves with slow, but deliberate movements.

JASON BOSLEY is extremely old and dressed in the turned collar of the minister. He speaks with a soft, almost ministerial quality in his voice. He wears silver-rimmed glasses.

EMILY JORDAN is perhaps the youngest of the four older people, but she is quite white-haired. Although she moves slowly as befits her age, she is the best preserved of the four. She has a good figure for one her age, dresses very well, and sports an up-to-date hairdo.

PHILIP MULLINS is even older than the other three. He is almost bent double with age but has an irresistible twinkle in his eye. His voice is cracked and slow as are his movements, but he has a wonderful sense of humor and is something of a flirt.

RICHARD COLLINS is about thirty and handsome in a more rugged than pretty-boy way. He has an air of sophistication from having worked in the city but he belongs to the easy-going life of the country.

JESSICA SELBY is a very attractive girl in her mid-twenties with a keen sense of humor, but capable of being extremely firm when the occasion arises.

HUBERT RATNER is middle-aged and smooth to the point of being almost oily. Being overly confident of himself, he considers his charm his biggest asset.

WARREN COATES is the same age as Hubert Ratner, but is the underdog. He always tries to please but has an unfortunate way of always saying the wrong thing.

FREDERICK RUGGLES is a pleasant-looking middle-aged man who shows great strength. His gruffness hides quite a warm heart.

SYLVIA COATES is the proper wife for a small town official. She is dressed extremely well, says the right thing, and is always conscious of her position.

NOTES ON THE PRODUCTION

A tremendous amount of the humor of "The Robin Hood Caper" is visual. Since the four "retired" crooks carry the bulk of the play, it is very important that the setting, props, costuming, etc., surround them in an aura of another era. They must be played in counterpoint to the lines they say. The more endearing and older the four of them are, the greater the humor. It is not vitally important as to how the age of the characters is played as long as they are individuals in their own right. The director should bear in mind that, even though the script calls for them to do a great deal of rushing around, they must move slowly and deliberately as befits their age. As noted in the script, the piano may easily be cut out if there is not available space. In this instance, the singing at the opening of Act Two can be done without accompaniment. If you bear in mind not to let the situations get out of hand and not to let the performances get too high in the more farcical scenes, you will have as successful a production as was the premier.

The Robin Hood Caper

ACT ONE

SCENE: *A living room in a large, old-fashioned house in Bridgeway Corners, Wisconsin. The furniture is old and contains several good antiques, the wallpaper is faded, the walls are heavily adorned with gold-framed paintings, some of them of people from another century. The windows have drapes and lace curtains. Up Center is a large archway with the front door opening Upstage Right in it. To the Left of the door a few steps lead Upstage to a landing and more steps go off the landing, Left. On the Left wall of the alcove is a closet door. In the living room itself, there is a pair of French windows Down Right, which open Offstage. Up Right is a window, and Down Left a door to the kitchen. Stage Right is a Victorian sofa with a small table to its Left and a tapestry rocking chair to the Left of it. Stage Left is a round table covered with a lace cloth, and three Victorian chairs around it. A recess in the Left wall contains a piano. Above the round table and against the wall is a small table containing a telephone and a lamp.*
NOTE: *The piano is not necessary, although it adds good business to the show.*

AT RISE: RICHARD COLLINS *is at the telephone facing Upstage in the middle of a conversation. He is about thirty and handsome in a pleasant sort of way. At the moment he is agitated.*

DICK. . . . just to tide me through. I'm in kind of a mess. (*Turns.*) I knew you made a killing on A T & T last January and I thought you could spare a little. . . . Of course, the income tax. I suppose you're in the ninety-percent bracket now. . . . Sure, Roger, I understand . . . Huntington Hartford, huh? . . . No, but I've tried everyone else. When I wrote that series of interviews for Redbook, every last famous person said to call them for help any time, but this seems to be the wrong time . . . Yeah, I'll let you know. Thanks. (*Hangs up, and bangs the phone lever for the operator.*) Operator, get me long distance, will you? (*Lights a cigarette.*) This is me again. Richard Collins in Bridgeway Corners. (*As if talking to a child.*) Yes, that's right. Wisconsin. I want to call Huntington Hartford. . . . That's right, the owner of the A & P. . . . No, not here in town, try New York City. I'll wait here but please hurry the call. (*Hangs up and paces to the window.*)

(*In a moment, a voice is heard from upstairs singing an old-fashioned song. It is* FLORY LANGLEY. *She is a very old and very kindly soul. Her manner and spirit are dripping with the milk of human kindness and there is an odd twinkle in her eye as she talks of her desire to help others. She dresses in very good clothes although somehow they aren't quite as fashionable as they might be. Being old, she moves with slow but deliberate movements.*)

DICK. It's a helluva morning to be singing.
FLORA. (*Comes downstairs carrying a sewing bag in which is a tapestry she works on and her instruction book.*) Good morning, Richard, dear.
DICK. Good morning, Auntie. (*They meet at Center and he kisses her on the cheek.*)
FLORA. I don't know why all the city people don't move out here—right to this spot.
DICK. Do you think we could handle the traffic?
FLORA. I mean it. (*Puts her work on the table Left.*) The view from my window is breath-taking. No one appreciates nature the way I do. I awoke this morning exactly at eight o'clock; (*Crosses to* RICHARD.) a quaint little bird was calling to his mate.

DICK. Auntie, that was the cuckoo clock.

FLORA. Well, I heard a starling answer. (*Moves to window.*) It's so beautiful here, Richard.

DICK. (*Smiling.*) Of course I agree with you, Auntie, or I wouldn't have given up the steaming metropolis for my Albert Schweitzer life.

FLORA. (*Crosses and gets her work, leaving the bag on the table.*) And everything *is* going all right for you, isn't it, Richard? I mean, the newspaper is a success?

DICK. Of course.

FLORA. (*Sits on the sofa and sews.*) Wherever I am, be it Bombay or Des Moines, the moment *The Clarion* comes in the mail, I sit right down, make a cup of tea, and read it from headlines to obituaries—even the ads. Except O'Connor's, of course.

DICK. (*Crosses below the rocking chair and flicks ash in ash tray on table by sofa.*) Don't you like their ad?

FLORA. There's something terribly sneaky about the way funeral parlors advertise. You always think it's an advertisement for a greenhouse the way they go on about lawns and shrubs and then they suddenly say you'll have a verdant eternal rest and I get sick.

DICK. (*Laughs and sits in chair.*) Mr. O'Connor is a very nice man.

FLORA. I'm sure he is. Well, as long as you like it here and the paper is a success, then all's right with the world. Your mother would be so proud of you. Not every man has the courage to start all over again the way you did.

DICK. It's just common sense. Most people get stuck in a rut and don't realize it until it's too late. Then they retire to somewhere like Bridgeway Corners. So I said to myself, "Richard, get to Bridgeway Corners while you're still young and can enjoy it." I'm sure the *Reader's Digest* gets along without me.

FLORA. I never did like that magazine. The moment you get interested in an article it's over. Like skim milk—the cream is gone.

DICK. (*Laughs.*) How about joining the staff of my paper as a critic?

FLORA. Goodness, no. I could never be a critic. I can't stand to hurt people's feelings. And, Richard, I hope your feelings won't be hurt but I moved that sweet little dresser scarf from the blue room into my room and put it on Emily's dresser. She'll love it.

DICK. The house came furnished. I wouldn't know a dresser scarf from a woolen muffler.

FLORA. There are some very nice pieces here. The house has a certain charm about it.

DICK. (*Crosses to the French windows and opens them, revealing the outside.*) You do whatever you want to make your friends comfortable.

FLORA. I'm especially anxious that Emily feel at home right away. This is her first time with us, you know. She's sort of going to take the place of Maude Burnley. Poor Maude, I'm going to miss her.

DICK. What did she die of?

FLORA. (*Stops her work.*) Heavens, she isn't dead. She's just— (*Starts on her work again.*) out of circulation. I do hope the others like Emily all right.

DICK. (*Sits on the sofa to the Right of* FLORA.) Auntie, I don't want to be the prying type, but exactly what does your little group do?

FLORA. Good works. We'll undertake any project we can that benefits mankind. We hate injustice and we've dedicated ourselves to fighting it.

DICK. It's a very noble purpose, I must say.

FLORA. Since the four of us are independently wealthy, so to speak, we can afford to spend our lives working for the happiness of others. You'll love the two men, Richard, I know you will. The Reverend Bosley is just the kindest man in the world. He's from Florida, you know. And Philip—that's Philip Mullins—well, generosity wouldn't melt in his mouth.

DICK. And this is your second meeting this year?

FLORA. Third. We went to St. Petersburg to the Reverend's for Christmas. But I didn't really care for it too much. You can't sing "Good King Wenceslaus" around Christmas balls hung on a palm frond. Then for Easter we went on a cruise to Bermuda. And now Bridgeway Corners. I must say, Richard, dear, it's very nice of you to let us come here.

DICK. It's the only way I'd ever get to see you. You're always so busy.

FLORA. There's a lot of sin in the world and it keeps us active. We could spend a whole year in Las Vegas and only scratch the surface.

DICK. (*Moves to the French windows.*) I really feel awful asking you to help out so much while you're here. I had planned to get a hired girl in, but it costs so much to rent the newspaper office and this house. Well, you know how it is.

FLORA. Nonsense. I love puttering about fixing up little foodstuffs.

DICK. I know you're used to having everything you want. Mother always read me your letters from Malaya when all you had to do was to clap your hands and servants came running.

FLORA. (*Goes to her sewing bag and gets out her instruction book.*) But they weren't very efficient. Never live on a rubber plantation, Richard. You can't escape the product. It's everywhere. I used to swear that everything bounced—even the servants. And hot! You could fry an egg in the ice box. (*Sits on the sofa and checks her sewing against the instructions in the book.*) To this day, I never see a rubber band that I don't break out in beads of perspiration.

DICK. (*Moves in to the Right of the sofa.*) Your letters always sounded so glamorous. Malaya seemed like the end of the world to me.

FLORA. (*Wryly.*) Me, too. But right here is heaven. Richard, you're so lucky, a thriving business, a beautiful house—

DICK. (*Crosses up to the window.*) It's a monstrosity for one person to rattle around in, but the bigger they are, the cheaper they come.

FLORA. It's gorgeous. Emily will just devour all the

antiques. And The Reverend—well, I don't know how we'll get any work done at all.

DICK. (*Moves Down Center.*) What work is there to do?

FLORA. Reports! We have to report to each other on what we've been doing and make suggestions on how we can improve our modus operandi as it were. You see, we all operate quite differently. We each have our specialty.

DICK. (*Sits in rocking chair.*) What is yours?

FLORA. Secrets of the organization, Richard; besides, you'd only be bored to death and think we were very silly. (*Obviously anxious to change the subject, she puts her work and instruction book in the bag and places the bag on the piano.*) Now, let's see, Emily's plane won't be in for a while yet. The men are taking the train. They're such scaredycats. And I have to run over next door and bring poor little Julia Lempkins some hot consomme. (*She crosses below the table towards the kitchen.*)

DICK. Julia Lempkins? You only got here yesterday. How'd you meet her so quickly?

FLORA. I haven't. The telephone operator told me she had a cold. And the best thing for a cold is home-made chicken consomme.

DICK. And when did you make that?

FLORA. I didn't, but you have some consomme cubes and I put some water on to heat. (*To the kitchen door.*) It may not be home-made, but it's the thought that counts. A little kindness brightens the corner where it's darkest before the dawn. (*She goes into the kitchen.* DICK *laughs. The PHONE rings and he rushes to it.*)

DICK. (*Into phone.*) Hello. . . . Yes, this is Richard Collins. . . . Put it through, please. . . . Hello, Hunt. . . . Oh, well where is he? . . . Visiting what? . . . Which A & P? When will he be back? . . . Down South in his private plane? . . . Oh, he got it with plaid stamps? . . . No, never mind, tomorrow is too late. Thanks anyway. (*Hangs up as* FLORA *comes in from kitchen carrying a Mason jar of chicken consomme.*)

FLORA. (*As she crosses to the French windows.*) There

we are. Nothing like a little chicken consomme for congestion. If any of the others come, just introduce yourself. Tell them I'm putting a little silver lining in a dark cloud. They'll understand. (*She goes out.*)

(*PHONE rings.*)

DICK. (*Into phone.*) Hello. . . . Oh, Jimmy. Yes, yes, I'll be down as soon as I can. The editorial is in the top right hand corner of the desk. You can set it up, but be careful. It's loaded. . . . No, nothing so far. I've got a call in to the New York bank. As soon as it comes through, I'll be down. (JESSICA SELBY *can be seen peeking in through the window.*) Yeah, so long. (*Hangs up and sits dejectedly in the rocking chair. The front door opens and* JESSICA *comes in. She is a very attractive girl in her mid-twenties with a keen sense of humor but capable of being very firm when she wants something. She is in a light summer dress. She sneaks up behind* DICK *and puts her hands over his eyes.*) Hey, what the—?

JESS. (*Kisses him.*) Guess who?

DICK. No one else in town would be this familiar. (*Takes her hand.*) Let's see—beautiful hands—one, two, three, four, five fingers. The usual amount. It must be Jessica Selby, girl beauty.

JESS. It is. (*Comes around and sits on his lap.*)

DICK. Good.

JESS. Want to try for a better kiss?

DICK. Um-hmm. (*Kisses her.*)

JESS. Oh, that *was* better. Time for another?

DICK. (*Pushes her up.*) No. (*Rises.*)

JESS. We are in a chilly frame of mind this morning, aren't we?

DICK. (*Moves below the sofa.*) I don't have time for this sort of thing.

JESS. I could go out on the road and see who I could pick up.

DICK. Be sensible. I'm waiting for the bank to call and that's my last hope.

Jess. (*Crosses to him.*) You can't be serious.

Dick. (*Pulls her onto the sofa next to him.*) I've tried to explain it to you in cold facts. I am going to lose the newspaper. I am going to be unemployed.

Jess. But *The Clarion* is a good paper. You've put it on the map.

Dick. I guess I never should have bought the thing in the first place. I should have stayed with the *Reader's Digest*—happy and abridged.

Jess. But you weren't happy.

Dick. A nine-to-five job and let other people do the worrying—that's the American way of life.

Jess. But it's not your way.

Dick. Why fight it? Why not join the monster and be another cog in the wheel of the big city?

Jess. Because I wouldn't have become engaged to a cog. (*Rises and moves to Center.*) If you want to marry some typical little cog's wife, you go right ahead.

Dick. The whole mess with the paper is my own fault because I went and got involved in a crusade. If I could just learn to mind my own business.

Jess. Great men always get involved in the lives of others. It's what makes heroes. Look at Abraham Lincoln and the slaves, Lawrence and the Arabians, Diamond Jim Brady and Lillian Russell.

Dick. (*Rises and moves to the window.*) You're trying to be funny.

Jess. (*Crosses to* Dick.) Darling, your spirit is what I love about you. Other people would just sit down and let Hubert Ratner get away with murder. But not you. You forge right ahead with typewriter keys flying. You're like one of those early pioneers hewing your way through the wilderness.

Dick. Jess, this is*n't* Guadalcanal. (*Moves to the Center of the table.*) All I did was write one little editorial on how Ratner was running the whole town and the explosion started. Now I'm going to lose the paper and also the mayoralty race.

Jess. Some people just aren't politicians.

DICK. (*Sits to Right of table.*) And I'm one of them.

JESS. (*Crosses to the piano.*) The nomination tickled you pink and you know it.

DICK. All I want is to see Mayor Ratner out of office and out of town and his sneaky little treasurer, Warren Coates, with him. (*Rises and moves above table towards* JESS.) Jess, you have no idea how they run Bridgeway Corners.

JESS. (*Leaning against the piano.*) You've told me often enough.

DICK. You can't get a taxi franchise in town unless you kick back to Ratner. Try to get a business license without slipping something under the Mayor's counter. If the stores don't kick in, the fire department declares them unsafe. (*Moves Center.*) Look what Ratner did with John's factory. I mean, how can an asbestos plant *not* be fireproof? (*Moves below the sofa.*) And what about the police cars? Ratner owns an automobile agency, so that's where the department gets new cars every year. I bet we're the only town in the United States that has Mercedes-Benz patrol wagons.

JESS. (*Crosses below the table.*) Sounds like the Riviera.

DICK. If I had it to do all over again, I'd just skip the editorials and run a society column.

JESS. (*Moves Center.*) You would not. You'd do just as you have done—get in there and fight him like Horace Greeley.

DICK. That kind of newspaper man went out with "The Front Page."

JESS. And there's no hope left other than the bank?

DICK. None. (*Sits on the sofa.*)

JESS. You can have what money I've saved. I don't need a Balenciaga wedding dress anyway.

DICK. No, this I do on my own. Win or lose, it's a Richard Collins enterprise. I still have till noon tomorrow before the option's up. Ratner's already put up a deposit to buy the building so I'll be out in the cold.

JESS. (*Sits next to him.*) Why can't you publish the paper right here? It's a big house.

DICK. In the first place, I couldn't afford to have the machinery moved, and in the second place, it's heavy. It would go right through the floor into the cellar and be flooded every spring. (*Crosses Center.*) Once again we see that the Amerircan way of life does not triumph.

JESS. How about your Aunt? She came last night, didn't she?

DICK. Yes.

JESS. Isn't she wealthy?

DICK. It's all tied up in annuities. She doesn't have any large capital to draw from. At least that's the way I understand it.

JESS. Don't you know?

DICK. (*During the following, he gives* JESS *a cigarette from his pocket, lights it, and takes one for himself.*) When you meet Aunt Flora, you'll see she's rather vague. Her husband left her a lot but not in a lump sum. He was a rubber planter in Malaya. She was away all the time I was growing up, but after he died, she came back to the States.

JESS. I just hope she approves of me.

DICK. How could she help it? (*PHONE rings.*) That's it. That's the bank.

JESS. Good luck. (*Crosses her fingers.*)

DICK. (*Into phone.*) Hello . . . yes, put it through, please . . . hello . . . yes, this is Mr. Collins . . . Oh, I see. I know there isn't much collateral, but . . . well, the circulation has increased since I took over . . . not possibly, huh? . . . I know you're sorry. So am I. . . . Yes . . . (*Starts to hang up, but pulls receiver back to his ear.*) What? . . . No, I don't need an auto loan. (*Hangs up.*)

JESS. No luck?

DICK. There goes the ball game. (*Crosses Center.*) Hell, I am mad! I am really mad!

JESS. (*Rises and moves in to Center. Worried.*) Don't start yelling, please. You know what will happen.

ACT I THE ROBIN HOOD CAPER 17

DICK. I don't give a damn what happens. All I want out of life is to run a small newspaper and look wha-wha-what happens. (*Starts stuttering.*)

JESS. Now be calm, dear.

DICK. (*Yells louder.*) Stop telling me to be calm. I have been ca-ca-calm all my l-l-life and I am sick to d-d-death of it.

JESS. See, you've started. (*Helps him to sofa. She remains above it.*) Lie down here. Put your feet up. And count to ten.

DICK. (*Calming down as he counts. He is lying on the sofa with his head towards Center.*) One, t-t-two, t-t-three, four, f-five, six . . .

JESS. There. That's better. You know, Dick, I think you ought to be psychoanalyzed.

DICK. (*Quite normal now.*) I am not insane.

JESS. Anyone who stutters every time he gets angry ought to be psychoanalyzed.

DICK. I know perfectly well why it happens. Some people break out in red blotches when they get angry. Some people throw up. I stutter. It's all my mother's fault.

JESS. It's silly to blame it on a woman.

DICK. (*Sits up.*) When I was a little boy, I was as excitable as Mother was calm. The bomb could have gone off and she wouldn't have raised her voice over a whisper. Whatever happened, she'd say, "Be calm." Then I'd have to count to ten and speak softly.

JESS. (*Sits Right of him.*) She sounds like a very wise woman.

DICK. It left me completely unprepared for manhood. I get all worked up to a lovely pitch of blowing off steam and then I stutter. It's very embarrassing. When I was overseas in Tokyo, they almost laughed me out of the service.

JESS. Why? Everyone has some little idiosyncrasy, doesn't he?

DICK. Not like mine. We all went to the Japanese baths where those doll-like girls scrub you and rub you down—with their bare feet. Everytime one of them would run up and down my back, I'd just go "da-da-da." Finally, they restricted me from the baths—it was bad for international relations. While all the other fellows were having fun there, I was on the post taking cold showers.

JESS. (*Laughs.*) Oh, Dick.

DICK. (*Crosses Center.*) It's not funny. And it's expensive. I lost fifty-five dollars and seventeen cents at one of those Elks' Bingo parties because by the time I had stuttered my way through yelling Bingo, three other people had collected the money, gone home, and the place was closed for the night.

JESS. There must be some way to get over it.

DICK. I just can't get excited or I have to lie down.

JESS. (*Moves to him.*) We're going to have a most peculiar wedding. When the minister asks you to say "I do," suppose you have to lie down before the altar.

DICK. (*Puts his arms around her.*) I'll take tranquilizers.

JESS. I had a friend—Rhoda Speegley. She stuttered, but they operated on her.

DICK. That's an idea.

JESS. Except it gave her a bass voice. She's got a wonderful job now. She dubs in Spencer Tracy's voice for foreign distribution.

FLORA. (*Enters from French windows.*) She loved the broth and never suspected a thing.

DICK. Good for you, Auntie. I'd like you to meet Jessica Selby. Jess, this is Mrs. Langley.

JESS. (*Crosses to* FLORA.) Dick's told me so much about you.

FLORA. How are you, my dear? (*They shake hands.*)

DICK. Incidentally, Jess is my fiancée.

FLORA. Fiancée? Richard, you have been keeping a surprise. Let me look at you, my dear. Ohhh, very nice. I don't know how you did it, Richard.

JESS. I swept him off his feet.

FLORA. Well, when is the wedding date? I won't want to miss that.

DICK. We haven't decided.

JESS. Very soon.

DICK. Not until several things have been ironed out.

JESS. Very soon!

FLORA. I'm with Jessica—very soon. (*She sits on the sofa.*)

DICK. You women certainly do gang up quickly, don't you? (JESS *sits in the rocking chair.*) You two get acquainted. I'd better get down to the paper and be sure Jimmy sets up the editorial correctly. (*Crosses to front door and opens it.*) He might be putting it on the obituary page which, as a matter of fact, might be very appropriate. (*He goes out, leaving the door open.*)

FLORA. Am I supposed to understand that?

JESS. I don't think so.

FLORA. Good. Now, my dear, tell me all about it. Where are you from?

JESS. Chicago.

FLORA. And how did you meet Richard?

JESS. Over the cottage cheese!

FLORA. Cottage cheese?

JESS. Uh-huh. I'm a phone operator. Long distance. And when Dick was in town he was always calling all over the country for the *Reader's Digest*. There was something about that voice that intrigued me.

FLORA. He takes after his father.

JESS. And then suddenly the timber went out of it, the thrill was gone. I was sure he must be dying of some strange malady so, on my day off, I just went and found him. He was sitting in the cafeteria eating cottage cheese and drinking skim milk.

FLORA. A great big man like that?

JESS. He had the beginnings of an ulcer. He needed someone to push him into getting off the big city merry-go-round and into doing what he wanted to, so I pushed. My uncle had just bought a summer place here, so I took Dick up here for a visit. He bought the paper and there we are, end of "My True Story." Little Jessica Found Love in the Printing Presses.

FLORA. Now, that is romantic.

JESS. Not like you. Dick tells me you used to live in Malaya.

FLORA. Yes, for a time when Richard was growing up. (*Crosses to the table and above it.*) But I don't like to talk about me. Just woman to woman, I want to ask you something rather personal. Is everything going all right with Richard? He doesn't seem his old self somehow.

JESS. (*Avoids the subject and crosses to the French windows.*) Sure. He's happy as a lark.

FLORA. My dear, you're lying, aren't you? You see—

EMILY. (*From outside the front door.*) Yoo-hoo. Flora?

FLORA. Emily. (*Starts up to door.*)

(EMILY JORDAN *enters carrying several suitcases and a hat box.* EMILY *is perhaps the youngest of the four older people in the play, but she is quite white-haired. Although she moves slowly, as befits her age, she is the best-preserved of the four. She has a good figure for one her age and is dressed very well and sports an up-to-date hairdo. She is wearing a hat, rather fussy, and a short fur jacket. She is very nervous and excited.*)

EMILY. Excuse me—oh, Flora. Then this *is* the right place. (*Puts the bags down Up Center.*)

FLORA. Emily, dear. You made it. (*She kisses* EMILY. JESSICA *fades up above the sofa.*) I'm so glad. Come right in. You must be exhausted after the plane trip.

EMILY. No, but I'm rather excited. And nervous.

FLORA. Emily, this is Jessica Selby, my nephew's fiancée. Jessica, I'd like you to meet Mrs. Jordan. She's going to be one of my best friends.

JESS. (*As they shake.*) Mrs. Jordan, nice to meet you.

EMILY. And Miss Selby—congratulations.

JESS. Thank you.

FLORA. Emily, we're sharing the same room. (EMILY *gives a little squeal of delight.*) And it has the most beautiful view. You'll be in seventh heaven. And the furniture! There's a genuine Hepplewhite imitation. With a little imagination, you'll think you're in Williamsburg.

EMILY. The men haven't come yet, have they?

FLORA. No. They're arriving by train. They should be here any minute.

EMILY. Good. I want to freshen up. I'm so nervous they won't like me. I feel just like a teenager at her first prom.

FLORA. (*To* JESS.) Emily is the new member of our club. (*Crosses to* JESS.) She's replacing Maude Burnley. She's gone but not forgotten.

JESS. I'm sorry. Did she die recently?

FLORA. She's not dead—just gone. She'll be back with us again.

JESS. (*Not understanding.*) Oh.

EMILY. Could I go up to the room for a minute?

FLORA. Of course. (*Moves to* EMILY'S *luggage.*) Let me help you.

EMILY. No. I can manage. I never travel with more than I can carry. You two go on with your visit. Just tell me where the room is.

FLORA. (*As she helps* EMILY *get hold of the luggage.*) Top of the stairs, turn right, and it's the first on the left. (EMILY *gets to the landing and* FLORA *moves to the Right of it.*) And, Emily, dear, do look at the dresser scarf. You'll have a vapor.

EMILY. Do you think this dress is all right? Not too showy?

FLORA. Nonsense, dear, you look lovely.

EMILY. (*As she goes upstairs.*) I hope I make a good impression. I don't want to seem too sexy.

FLORA. (*Moves to above the table.*) Poor soul, she shouldn't be so nervous. The men are both angels.

JESS. (*Sits Right of the table.*) Exactly what do you do at your gatherings, Mrs. Langley?

FLORA. We discuss new ways we've found of helping

others, new charities that are deserving of our attention. (*Sits above the table.*) We get together and devote our shadow years to helping others.

JESS. Sounds terribly noble.

FLORA. Heavens, no. We all have skeletons in our closets that would give our nobility feet of clay.

JESS. Maybe if you started your works in your own backyard—

FLORA. You mean Richard?

JESS. Yes. As I was going to tell you, he—

(JASON BOSLEY'S *face appears at the window. He calls back behind him.* JASON *is extremely old and dressed in the turned collar of the minister. He speaks with a soft, almost ministerial quality to his voice. He wears silver rimmed glasses. Enters with two suitcases.*)

JASON. (*Calling back to* PHILIP.) It's the right house number, Philip.

FLORA. (*Rises and starts for door.*) Jason.

JASON. (*As he enters.*) My dear Flora, we have found you. (*Calls back to* PHILIP.) Yes, Philip, this is it. (*Puts his suitcases down.* JESSICA *rises and fades below the table.*) A charming place for our meeting, Flora; you are to be congratulated.

FLORA. I got here last night. I've been so anxious for you to arrive. (PHILIP MULLINS *enters also carrying two suitcases. He wears a topcoat.* PHILIP *is perhaps even older than the other three. He is almost bent double with age but has a wonderful twinkle in his eye. His voice is cracked and slow, as are his movements, but he has a wonderful sense of humor. He wears a dark suit.*) Philip, dear, how wonderful to see you again. (*Crosses to him and indicates his stomach.*) I do believe you've put on weight.

PHILIP. It's age, my dear, just age.

JASON. (*Descends on* JESSICA *with outstretched hand.*) And this must be our new member. I am delighted to meet you. (*Shakes her hand.*) I am sure we will work beautifully together.

FLORA. No, no, no, Jason. This is Jessica Selby, my nephew's fiancée. Emily Jordan is upstairs.

JASON. A thousand pardons. Allow me. I am the Reverend Jason Bosley and this is Philip Mullins.

JESS. How do you do? (PHILIP *gives her a little wave indicating he has noticed she is an attractive woman.*)

JASON. A charming girl, Flora. Your nephew is fortunate.

PHILIP. Miss Selby, I'm pleased to meet you.

JESS. (*Crosses to front door.*) I think I'd better run down to the newspaper office and visit with Dick. I'm sure you want to reminisce and gossip.

FLORA. All right, dear. Tell Richard they all arrived and they just adore the house.

JESS. I will. See you all later. (*Goes out and closes the front door.*)

FLORA. (*As* PHILIP *removes his topcoat.*) I'm so anxious for you to meet Emily. I'm sure she'll work out beautifully. Of course we'll miss Maude, there's no two ways about it. Such a good worker—but careless.

JASON. I am bursting to tell you about all my new projects.

FLORA. (*Taking* PHILIP's *coat from him.*) But first go upstairs and leave your bags.

PHILIP. Let's not even unpack. Let's meet right away.

FLORA. As you wish. You two are at the top of the stairs and to the left. First door.

JASON. (*As they start upstairs with their luggage.*) A beautiful haven. The entire world should be so peaceful.

PHILIP. I'm sure we can get some really good work done here. (*They are off.*)

FLORA. (*Calling after them.*) If you go into the bathroom, knock first. I don't want you to meet Emily under anything but the most auspicious conditions. (*Hangs the coat up in the closet. To herself.*) Oh, and I'll make some tea. (*She starts for the kitchen as* EMILY *rushes downstairs.*)

EMILY. (*From the landing.*) Flora.

FLORA. Yes, Emily, dear.

EMILY. The men are here. I heard their voices. (*Comes off stairs.*) They came upstairs and I hid in the linen closet.

FLORA. Emily, dear.

EMILY. There's the most wonderful damask dinner cloth in there. I'm so nervous. Do you think they'll like me?

FLORA. (*Crosses to* EMILY *and pats her hand.*) Of course they will, dear. After all, we have the same common denominator—we work for charity.

EMILY. (*Suddenly grabs* FLORA'S *shoulders.*) Whatever happens, Flora, I want you to know that I appreciate all you've done for me. (*Slowly pivots.*) You really think this dress is all right?

FLORA. Stunning, Emily. I wish I had your figure.

EMILY. (*Puts her purse on the sofa table.*) Three times a year I go on a diet. Nothing for a week but kumquats, and then on the eighth day, one saltine. It works wonders. (PHILIP *and* JASON *come downstairs.* PHILIP *carries a briefcase.*) Are my seams straight? (EMILY *leans over to adjust her stockings. She faces the audience and her back is to the stairs.*)

FLORA. (*Fades above the table.*) Straight as the stare of a glass eye.

JASON. (*As he catches his first sight of* EMILY *bent over.*) Ah, this must be our new member.

EMILY. (*Freezes in position.*) Oh, gracious me! (*She straightens up.*)

FLORA. Emily Jordan, it gives me great pleasure to introduce the Reverend Jason Bosley.

EMILY. How do you do?

JASON. Charmed, my dear.

FLORA. And Philip Mullins.

PHILIP. My pleasure.

FLORA. Richard and his fiancée are out, so let's sit right down and get acquainted over a nice hot cup of Orange Pekoe. (*She starts for the kitchen.*)

EMILY. (*As she sits on the rocking chair.*) First, let me say that I appreciate the way you've let me barge in like this. If you don't feel I'll fit in, just say the word and I'll gladly withdraw.

JASON. (*As he sits to the Right of the table.*) Beautifully put. Did you ever write?

EMILY. Heavens no. That was never my specialty.

PHILIP. (*As he sits on the sofa still carrying his briefcase with him.*) Modesty forbids me telling you the extent of my credits as an author.

(*They* ALL *laugh except* EMILY.)

FLORA. Oh, Philip. (*She goes into kitchen.*)

EMILY. I never dreamed there was such a club as this, that people could meet and talk over ways to make others happy. It's so tremendously Faith Baldwin.

FLORA. (*Comes in holding kettle full of water.*) First, I think we should all vote on whether to accept Emily into Charities Anonymous. Let me say that, since becoming acquainted with Emily, I have grown to love her not only as a person but as a great humanitarian, a sort of budding Aimee Semple McPherson.

EMILY. Thank you, Flora.

FLORA. Don't mention it, dear. I would like to go on record as saying that I investigated Emily thoroughly before daring to mention our organization and then I did it most slyly with the merest thrust of a verb here and a noun there. She bit like a catfish for a worm. Then, when it became apparent dear Maude was going to be—out of the picture for a few years, it seemed as if fate had sent Emily to us. But before we vote on her, Philip, as acting secretary, would you please read our charter.

PHILIP. Delighted. (*Takes rolled parchment from his briefcase. Rises and takes a reading magnifying glass from his jacket pocket. Reads.*) "It is the pleasure of Charities Anonymous—" (FLORA *goes into the kitchen.*) "to do whatever we can to spread joy to those more unfortunate than ourselves. We have all sinned grievously and in so doing have learned a trade which turned the world against us. Having paid for errors, we now turn our trade towards helping others. By whatever means at our command, we of Charities Anonymous shall brighten everyone's corner wherever he is." (*Almost overcome*, PHILIP *sits*.)

FLORA. (*Re-enters with tea bag in hand.*) Isn't that beautiful, dear?

EMILY. (*Choked up.*) Inspiring. (FLORA *exits to kitchen.*)

JASON. I wrote it.

PHILIP. You authored it, Jason. I wrote it down. It was reminiscent of the Gettysburg Address, I felt, so I penned it in the handwriting of Honest Abe. (*Shows it to* EMILY.) See?

EMILY. Amazing.

PHILIP. And that was a rush job. You should see me when I really work over something. (*Puts document back in briefcase, which he leaves Left of sofa.*)

JASON. Of course I feel we all owe our start to Frederick Ruggles.

EMILY. Rugged Ruggles?

JASON. Then you know him?

EMILY. Of course. He sent me up, too.

JASON. When I first met him, he was acting Police Commissioner of Chicago and I didn't take too kindly to him.

FLORA. (*Enters with tray of cups, saucers, sugar and creamer. Puts them on the table to serve above table.*) I thought he was a dreadful man. But after I was released and had to check in at the parole board every Tuesday, we became very good friends. At that time he was just beginning as parole officer. Those chats of his were so heartening.

PHILIP. He even reached me. And, believe me, there was no one who was so dead set against honesty as I. But there was something so inspiring about him that—well, you see what I'm doing now. (*Pats the briefcase.*)

FLORA. I'd be so full of love when I left the parole

office that I'd go next door to that little tea shoppe—"The Golden Earring"—and leave a quarter tip for a ten cent cup of tea.

PHILIP. That was where we all met. "The Golden Earring."

JASON. They tore it down last year. Now it's a home for wayward girls.

FLORA. (*Crosses to above* JASON *and puts a hand on his shoulder.*) I remember so well the first time I saw you, Jason. So distinguished sitting there buttering your crumpet.

JASON. I wasn't a reverend then. I was usually a banker in those days.

FLORA. He smiled at me and I thought he was a masher. But as the weeks went by, every Tuesday Jason would be there buttering and I'd be dunking my tea bag. (*Moves towards* EMILY.) Finally, we got to chatting. We had so much in common. True, we'd been to different prisons, but then we'd both been apprehended by Rugged Ruggles and both been released at the same time.

PHILIP. Then I came along.

FLORA. (*Starts for kitchen.*) My water must be boiling. (*Turns in doorway.*) Oh, Philip, tell dear Emily how you introduced yourself. (*Laughs as she goes into the kitchen.*)

PHILIP. It was very embarrassing really. You see, I'd been watching Flora and Jason for weeks having such a nice time together and finally I decided to introduce myself. I went over to their table and said, "How do you do?" They asked me to sit down and told me their names. And I said—oh, I could have died a thousand deaths—"I'm pleased to meet you. My name is 297365."

JASON. Right away we knew he was one of us.

FLORA. (*Enters from kitchen with full tea pot. It is under a tea cozy.*) And when I found out Emily had been caught by Rugged Ruggles, too, I just knew it was providence. (*Moves above table and puts down pot.*) I explained that, having changed our ways, we now look upon ourselves as Robin Hoods. We take from the rich and give to the poor. (*Takes off cozy.*) Tea, dear?

EMILY. Please.

JASON. So we meet two or three times a year and report on our good works. Of course we can never expect to gain public recognition, since often we have to resort to the unusual means in which we were so well trained to gain our ends. But then goodness is its own reward.

FLORA. Sugar and cream, dear?

EMILY. Nothing. I have my saccharin with me.

FLORA. (*Crosses Center with tea.*) Oh, that divine figure. Isn't it lovely, gentlemen?

EMILY. (*As the* MEN *turn to her.*) Flora, please.

FLORA. (*Hands tea to* EMILY *and crosses Center.*) I remember the day it all started. We three had left the tea shoppe along with poor Maude. There was a blind man begging on the corner. We each put a quarter in his tin cup and then this mink-clad woman rushed by us so fast she almost pushed me through the window of Chung Ling's Chinese Laundry. But she had dropped a diamond bracelet.

JASON. I picked it up and was about to call after her when Flora put her hand over my mouth.

FLORA. (*Moves above table.*) There was this poor, bedraggled beggar without a penny in the world and there was this rich woman. Who needed the diamonds more? We dropped the bracelet into his tin cup.

PHILIP. Didn't he deserve it? Anyway the woman was obviously insured.

FLORA. We had taken the liberty of balancing the weights of wealth. Of course one has to be careful to whom one gives charity. I'm casting no aspersions on the beggar, but he lifted his dark glasses, said "Geez! It's real!" and ran. But the principle was there. Tea, Jason? (*Pours cup.*)

JASON. Sugar and cream, please.

PHILIP. It was apparent our mission in life was to spread the wealth. Of course we all had independent incomes from money we had stashed away prior to our confinement. (FLORA *hands tea to* JASON.)

JASON. So we decided to use our trades to help others. (FLORA *pours another tea.*)

FLORA. Except in the spring. We give it up for Lent. Sugar, Philip?

PHILIP. I think I'll try one of Mrs. Jordan's saccharin if I may?

EMILY. My pleasure. (FLORA *takes tea to* PHILIP. EMILY *drops a pill in as it goes by. Then* FLORA *hands tea to* PHILIP *and moves below sofa.*)

JASON. Now, Flora, tell us how you met up with Mrs. Jordan.

EMILY. Please, Reverend, call me Emily.

JASON. If you'll call me Jason. (EMILY *looks to* FLORA *who nods approval.*) The Reverend part is new. I've been so many people in my lifetime, but the ministry seems to fit me best. People are so polite to me just because my collar is reversed. To think that such a simple thing as the way one wears one's clothes can determine the courtesy of others.

FLORA. You put things so well, Jason. I wonder if we could have you deliver a guest sermon in the church on Sunday.

JASON. I'd be delighted.

FLORA. (*Moves Up Center above the sofa.*) Well, I met Emily in Chicago. I'd just come out of the Keith where I had seen a rerun of "Little Caesar" and "Public Enemy." I knew so many of those boys. I noticed Emily walking down the street. I can spot one of us a mile off— there's something about the set of the shoulders and the straight walk one gets used to during recreation hour in the pen. So I slipped into the doorway of a drugstore and watched her. You know what she was doing? (*Moves by* EMILY *and puts her hands on her shoulders. Delighted.*) She was emptying all the parking meters! (*The* MEN *nod in appreciation and surprise.*)

EMILY. (*Modestly.*) My mother taught me to save a nickel by using a hairpin to get into the ladies' toilets.

FLORA. I followed her for three blocks.
EMILY. Then I dropped my hairpin down a drain.
FLORA. So I offered her one of mine.
EMILY. I was petrified. I thought she was a woman policeman.
FLORA. She'd done so well that night, her satchel was overflowing. I helped her carry it back to her place where she fixed us a nice cup of hot chocolate with two marshmallows. I knew she was our type when she told me she was collecting the meter money to contribute to the March of Dimes.
JASON. Ingenious.   PHILIP. How thoughtful.
FLORA. (*Starts for kitchen.*) I bet I can find some cookies out there if I look. (*Exits.*)
EMILY. But now I want to do really big things to make up for my past mistakes. I don't want to stop at dimes. I want to give thousands.
JASON. Tell us, Emily, what was your racket?
EMILY. Husbands.
PHILIP. Husbands?
EMILY. I collected them. In my day, of course, I was something of a knockout. When I went to jail, the *Daily News* dubbed me "The Lillian Russell of the Thirties."
PHILIP. Why did you collect husbands?
EMILY. Oh, alimony, insurance, army benefits. At one time, back in the late twenties, I had seventeen husbands supporting me.
JASON. An inspiring story.
FLORA. (*Enters with plate of cookies. She crosses Center.*) Here we are. Oatmeal cookies or Grandma Gloria's Fudge Wafers. Of course, I've told Emily all about me. In my day, there was nothing these ten little fingers couldn't lift. They were like tiny magnets. I'd do the stores in the morning, the subways in the afternoon, and the theatres at night. They used to call me "Fingers Langley." (*To* EMILY.) Cookie, dear?
EMILY. Thank you.
FLORA. (*Moves above sofa and passes cookies to* PHILIP.) My big mistake came at a large Christmas din-

ner. I was being a maid at the time. While serving the avocado, I spied a gorgeous pair of cufflinks on a man's sleeve. (*Moves Center.*) At the time I was keeping company with a bootlegger called Stills Malone and I thought they'd look marvelous on him. But it was not to be. They were on the sleeve of Rugged Ruggles. That was the last avocado I laid eyes on for eighteen years. (*Passes plate to* JASON.) Cookie, Jason?

JASON. One of the fudge wafers, I believe.

FLORA. But now I use my fingers to do good. I lift from the rich and then drop their jewels in the slums right in front of some deserving soul. (*Sits above the table and pours her own tea.*)

PHILIP. I, on the other hand, Emily, started very young. I was always artistic. My mother used to call me her little Rembrandt. But colors never attracted me— only black and white thin straight lines like signatures. (*Rises and moves to the cookie plate for another.*) When I was still in grade school, I started selling genuine autographed books to my classmates.

EMILY. What books?

PHILIP. All of Mark Twain, personally autographed by Tom Sawyer. For twenty-five cents additional, I'd throw in Huck Finn.

JASON. I'm glad you never tried the Bible.

PHILIP. (*Moves to Center.*) But I was fourteen when something happened that determined my life's work. I saw my first checkbook. Oh, the worlds of signatures to copy. I loved every squiggle and loop of them.

EMILY. Of course. You're the one who sold Napoleon's letters to Josephine for twenty-three thousand dollars.

PHILIP. One of my minor efforts.

JASON. That is all in the past, Philip. Tell Emily of your brilliant charity work of the present.

PHILIP. It's really exquisite. I send in a sizable check from some well-known person to a charitable organization. When the check appears on his bank statement, what can he do? Does he dare say the check is a fake and that his generosity is not genuine? Of course not. He smiles and pays. I work a sort of enforced contribution system. (*Crosses to sofa.*) In all modesty, I must say I'm responsible for the new children's wing on the Detroit hospital. (*Sits.*)

EMILY. You make my measly efforts seem so pitiful.

FLORA. More tea, anyone? (ALL *turn it down.*) Then I think we should vote. Now, all in favor of accepting Emily Jordan into Charities Anonymous, so signify.

ALL. Aye.

FLORA. We welcome you, Emily.

EMILY. (*Pulls out handkerchief.*) I'm so deeply touched that— (*She stifles tears.*)

JASON. (*Crosses to* EMILY *and pats her shoulder.*) There. There. It is our pleasure.

(*Front DOORBELL rings.*)

FLORA. Oh-oh. Company. (*She rises and starts for front door.* JASON *fades to above the sofa.*) Oh, Emily, dear, in case Richard ever asks, I always told him I was in Malaya with a husband when I was really—well, you know, away. I'm not asking you to lie, dear. I wouldn't do that. Just be evasive. (*Opens the front door and* HUBERT RATNER *and* WARREN COATES *are talking to each other.* HUBERT RATNER *is middleaged and smooth. He is confident of himself and considers his charm his biggest asset.* WARREN COATES *follows* RATNER, *always at his heel. He is the same age and is inclined to put his foot in it by saying the wrong thing.*) Yes?

RATNER. (*Gruffly.*) I want to— (*Turns and sees* FLORA *and all his charm oozes forth.*) Oh, I beg your pardon, but is Mr. Collins in?

FLORA. Not at the moment. He's down at the newspaper. Who shall I say called?

RATNER. (*As he steps in.*) Hubert Ratner. (*Sees the* OTHERS.) Mayor Hubert Ratner.

FLORA. Oh, we're honored. I'm Mrs. Langley, Richard's aunt.

RATNER. (*Worried.*) Yes, he's often spoken of his wealthy relatives.

FLORA. Won't you come in?

RATNER. Thank you. This is the town treasurer, Warren Coates. (WARREN *enters into the room.*)

FLORA. How do you do?

WARREN. Mrs. Langley.

FLORA. (*Fades to above the table.*) This is Mrs. Jordan, The Reverend Bosley, and Philip Mullins. (*They exchange greetings as the* MEN *sit on the sofa.*) We're old friends. Won't you have a cup of tea?

COATES. (*Recoiling at the thought.*) Tea!

RATNER. No, thank you. (*Crosses to* FLORA.) This little visit of yours, is it—er—are you going to help Richard with his business?

FLORA. Goodness, no, we're not business people. (*Sits.*) Just retired fuddy-duddies doing our little bit in the world.

RATNER. Good.

FLORA. Besides, how could I help Richard? He's doing very well, isn't he?

WARREN. If you call losing the paper doing well.

RATNER. (*With a scathing look at* WARREN.) Warren!

FLORA. Losing the paper?

RATNER. (*All charm.*) Now, now, Mrs. Langley. It's just a matter of business. Nothing you would be interested in.

FLORA. But if Richard is in trouble—

DICK. (*Comes in.*) Well, well, well, if it isn't our mayor!

RATNER. I wanted to see you, Mr. Collins. I hardly thought you'd be at your office.

DICK. Let's go down there now. I don't like to discuss business in front of guests.

FLORA. (*Rises.*) Oh, how impolite of me. Richard, I'd like to present Mrs. Jordan, The Reverend Bosley—

JASON. My son.

FLORA. And Philip Mullins. This is my nephew, Richard Collins. His mother wanted to call him Tom but she was a teetotaler.

DICK. I must apologise for the mayor bursting in here.

FLORA. On the contrary, we've been having a most illuminating chat. He's been telling me about your troubles. I think he's here to help you.

DICK. That's a laugh. He owns the building the paper is in and he's throwing me out tomorrow at noon.

RATNER. Not throwing out, Mrs. Langley, let me assure you, merely concluding a business arrangement. Your nephew is unable to pay his bills, so that's that.

DICK. I've tried to negotiate a loan, you know that, Ratner. All I wanted was a week's extension.

RATNER. Tomorrow at noon!

FLORA. I'm sure something can be worked out.

DICK. Not with our honest mayor.

RATNER. (*Losing his temper*.) Now just a minute—

DICK. (*Moves below* RATNER *to* FLORA.) It seems the mayor is scared of my editorials. I tell too much. I know you wouldn't understand this, Auntie, but the men would. (*To the* OTHERS.) Our Mayor is getting rich off this town by graft. That's a sort of bribery.

PHILIP. We're acquainted with the word.

DICK. And I've been exposing him in the paper. Now the decent citizens of the town are trying to put me up for mayor.

RATNER. I've tried to be friendly, Mr. Collins, but I see it's to no avail. So tomorrow at noon, you get out! If you don't, I'll throw your machinery out in the street. Right, Coates?

WARREN. I agree, Mayor. (*To* DICK.) Why don't you move into the city? There's a lot more to expose there. Here we only dabble in *petty* graft.

RATNER. Shut up, Coates.

DICK. I happen to like a small town. I like the life here, I like the people here. Ratner, it's time someone told you off once and for all. You are a louse. You are a dirty, grafting, petty pol-pol-politician. Excuse me, I have to lie down. (*He heads for the sofa. The* MEN *rise and back Right.* DICK *lies down.*) No one has the right to r-r-run a t-t-town and fur-fur-furthermore—

RATNER. If you can't stand up like a man, don't try to talk like one. I shall see you tomorrow at noon. Come along, Coates. (*Starts for door.*)

PHILIP. Just a minute. Mayor, would you give me your autograph. (*To* JASON.) I think it may come in handy.

RATNER. Send twenty-five cents to the Town Hall and you'll get a signed photograph. (*He exits.*)

WARREN. (*Starts out, comes back and speaks to* PHILIP.) Mine are only fifteen cents. (*He runs off after* RATNER.)

DICK. Oh, hell!

JASON. A shocking man. I hope he never comes to me to make his confession. It would take too long. (*Looks out after them.*)

PHILIP. (*Crosses Down Right.*) In Chicago in the twenties, he would be wearing a concrete kimono by nightfall.

FLORA. (*Moves next to* EMILY.) I wish I could help, Richard, dear, but my money is all tied up in investments.

DICK. (*Slowly sits up.* JASON *moves to above the table.*) Now, this isn't your problem, any of you. You know nothing of graft and crime.

JASON. Ohhhhh, word gets around!

FLORA. What are you going to do, Richard?

DICK. (*Goes Center.*) There's nothing to do but go back down to the office and write one final editorial for tomorrow's edition and hope it does some good. If all the people in town would just stand up against him once, he'd be licked.

FLORA. Don't get angry, dear; you know you stutter.

DICK. Not on my typewriter. (*He goes out front door.*)

JASON. What a pity that sin has spread even to this heavenly town.

PHILIP. He reminds me of a roommate I had in Alcatraz.

EMILY. I know I shouldn't butt in. You're all more experienced in this than I, but it does seem to me that

Mayor Ratner is guilty morally. Wouldn't it be considered a good work to save the newspaper for Richard and get him elected mayor?

(*The* OTHERS *slowly turn to* EMILY *and nod sagely.*)

FLORA. I call an emergency meeting of Charities Anonymous. All in favor?
ALL. Aye. (PHILIP *sits on the sofa,* JASON *above the table.*)
FLORA. Are we agreed it is a project of the organization to take from Mayor Ratner and give to Richard?
ALL. Aye.
FLORA. Is it agreed this must be done immediately if not sooner?
ALL. Aye.
FLORA. Then let's figure out how to do it. (FLORA *sits in chair Right of table and she and* JASON *start a heated discussion.* PHILIP *and* EMILY *are talking rapidly. Plans are well under way as:*)

The CURTAIN falls

ACT TWO

TIME: *After dinner that evening.*

BEFORE RISE: *The voices of* FLORA, EMILY, JASON, *and* PHILIP *are heard singing.*

ALL.
>Rock of Ages
>Cleft for me
>Let me hide myself in thee.

AT RISE: *MOONLIGHT shines in through windows.* JASON *is at the piano.* FLORA *is sitting in the rocking chair doing her tapestry.* EMILY *is sitting on the sofa reading a movie magazine.* PHILIP *is sitting Right of the table, his briefcase on the floor beside him. He is writing a letter and has an envelope before him.* DICK *is not singing, but is looking out the French windows and smoking.*

ALL.
>Let the water and the blood
>From thy riverside which flowed
>Be of sin the double cure
>Cleanse me from its guilt and power.

FLORA. Beautiful, Jason. (JASON *moves his chair back to the Left of the table and resumes playing solitaire.*)

PHILIP. (*After a moment during which he signs a letter.*) Strange.

FLORA. What is?

PHILIP. Barbara Hutton has two "t's" in her name. I always thought it was one.

FLORA. That would make it Huton.

PHILIP. Did you know she's vitally interested in sending missionaries to Tanganyika? (*Puts letter in envelope.*)

FLORA. No.

PHILIP. (*Licks envelope and presses down flap.*) Well, she is!

EMILY. (*After a pause, looks up from magazine.*) I don't see why they get so excited about Elizabeth Taylor having so many husbands. After all, she had them one at a time.

FLORA. She's too flagrant, dear. It takes great finesse to carry that sort of thing off properly.

EMILY. (*Pleased.*) Thank you. That's a beautiful pattern, Flora. Oriental, isn't it?

FLORA. Honestly, I don't know. I was walking through Marshall Fields' one day and I picked it up.

EMILY. You mean—?

FLORA. No. I bought it. (*The* TWO WOMEN *giggle.*)

JASON. (*Looks around then pulls a card from his sleeve.*) Ah-ha! Won again. I am infallible.

DICK. (*Turns from window and comes in above sofa.*) Don't forget, there's plenty of cold turkey left if any of you want a sandwich before you go to bed.

JASON. Thank you, Richard, but that was a huge dinner. I don't think I'll ever eat again.

DICK. It was wonderful of you ladies to pitch in and cook like that.

EMILY. My mother used to say the way to a man's heart was through his stomach. And it works—always. I remember once cooking suki-yaki for a Japanese prince— (FLORA *gives a warning clearing of her throat.*) but that's a long story.

DICK. We had a wonderful Japanese restaurant on the outskirts of town, but it had to move.

EMILY. Why?

DICK. It was condemned. Unsanitary kitchen.

EMILY. All the Japanese I know are extremely clean.

DICK. (*Crosses Center.*) So was this one, but he didn't kick in to Ratner, so now he's opened up over in Middletown.

FLORA. It's really as bad as that?

DICK. Worse. Of course Ratner's doing everything le-

ACT II   THE ROBIN HOOD CAPER   39

gally with me, but if I hadn't started my exposé, I wouldn't be thrown out tomorrow. Something's got to happen! (*Crosses up to the open front door and looks out.*)

(*The* OTHERS *slowly realize what* DICK *has said and turn to one another and nod.*)

FLORA. Don't worry, Richard. I'm sure something will.
DICK. (*Comes back Center.*) I'm just kidding myself.
JASON. Have a little faith.
FLORA. People always come to the aid of their fellow man when he's in trouble.
DICK. (*Puts cigarette out at telephone table.*) You have a wonderful philosophy, Aunt Flora.
FLORA. Something I picked up when I was sent away— to Malaya! (EMILY *gives her a look.*)
DICK. But this isn't a small charity problem. To get Ratner out of office, it will take nothing short of murder. (*Crosses to window and looks out. The* OTHERS *stare front a moment, then turn to each other with a diabolical gleam in their eyes.*)
JASON. No, no. That's going too far.
DICK. (*Turning.*) I beg your pardon.
JASON. Nothing, my son. Just thinking out loud.
FLORA. Don't you have to go down to the office, Richard? You mentioned it during dinner.
DICK. In a minute. Don't pay any attention to me, you go right ahead and have your meeting.
FLORA. Secrecy, dear. We never let the outside world infringe when we get down to work. Unfortunately, one has to concentrate very hard to do good.
DICK. (*Kisses the top of her head and crosses Up Center.*) Aunt Flora, you're one in a million. All right, I'll go finish the paper and then we'll sit down and have a farewell drink to the *Bridgeway Corners Clarion*.
FLORA. You can drink but, if you don't mind, we'll just have some cocoa.
DICK. You know, it's heartening that there are still

people like you four in the world. Innocence is a wonderful thing. Stay just as you are. The meek shall inherit the earth. (*He goes out leaving the door open.* PHILIP *goes up, looks after him and closes the door.*)

JASON. I said the same thing once, but the judge didn't think I was meek enough and I got five years.

PHILIP. He's gone. (*Crosses and sits Right of table.*)

FLORA. Let's get to work.

EMILY. This is exciting. We find a project our first evening together and one we can do right here.

PHILIP. Much better than by mail.

JASON. (*Rises and moves to below table.*) I feel the old excitement coming back. The tingling, the thrill of the chase.

EMILY. Jason, what was your specialty? You never said.

JASON. Perhaps you may be acquainted with me under my nom de crime—"The Chameleon?"

EMILY. Of course. They used to talk about you in prison. You were sort of an idol. You had a marvelous write-up in True Detective last year.

JASON. It almost ruined me. (*Crosses Center.*) Thank heavens, I've aged since those photographs were taken and look quite different now. Ah, I always felt the stage was my forte. But the unemployment lines discouraged me and so I found a better outlet for my histrionics. The parts I've played to perfection. Bank guards, bonded messengers, and all with such a deft touch. But the characterization that fits me best you see before you. The retired minister. On occasion, of course, I do doff it and step out. Last season, I was a wealthy Texas oilman who stopped off in Miami and got involved in a few card games, another specialty of mine. By the time I left the Beach, I had contributed sixteen thousand, three hundred and forty-two dollars of other people's money to an orphan's home.

FLORA. Jason, you're wasting time. We have a job to do. My adrenalin glands are fairly popping with excitement. I haven't felt this way since the time in Atlantic

City when I removed Miss America's crown in the ladies lounge.

JASON. (*Moves above sofa.*) I believe, in the modern parlance of the underworld, they call this type of job a caper.

PHILIP. That's the new word?

EMILY. Caper? Like you put in your salad?

JASON. (*Crosses to Right of sofa.*) That's right.

FLORA. (*Rises, crosses to piano and puts her sewing bag there.*) I hereby call Charities Anonymous to order. Before dinner this evening, we agreed it was a project of ours to save this town and one Richard Collins from Mayor Ratner and his henchman, Warren Coates. Right?

ALL. Right. (JASON *sits to the Left of the sofa.*)

FLORA. It was further agreed, after several plans were discussed and discarded, that we should use the old blackmail formula.

ALL. Agreed.

FLORA. However, since we don't know Mayor Ratner personally or any scandal about him, it is our job this evening to create some incident that will give reason for blackmail and before noon tomorrow. A challenging problem to say the least.

EMILY. I would gladly offer my services in matrimony but I'm too old now to expect success in *one* evening.

FLORA. It must be an immediate situation. (*Moves Center.*)

PHILIP. If I had his autograph, there's no telling what I could have him sign.

JASON. I'm afraid we're still back to the original thought—blackmail by murder.

EMILY. As long as no one will get hurt.

PHILIP. (*Rises and crosses to* FLORA.) It's one of the oldest and safest ruses ever invented in the twisted minds of criminals.

FLORA. I don't like that "twisted minds" so much.

PHILIP. It's what authors always say.

JASON. (*Crosses to* FLORA'S *Right.*) We're wasting time. Now who shall Mayor Ratner murder? (*Looks at*

FLORA, *who turns to* PHILIP *who turns to his Left. Then they all turn to* EMILY.)

EMILY. (*Smiles weakly.*) I'm gun-shy, but I'll gladly work with a knife.

JASON. I have always been considered something of a good actor. I'm sure I could arrange an effective death scene.

PHILIP. You'd ham it up. (*Sits above table.*)

JASON. (*Withering him with a look.*) I beg your pardon.

PHILIP. Let's draw cards.

JASON. An excellent idea. (*Crosses above* PHILIP.)

PHILIP. But no cheating.

JASON. (*Stops moving.*) Philip, you shouldn't speak that way to a man of the cloth. (*Gets his cards from Left of the table.*) I happen to have some cards right here. (*Shuffles them.*) Shall we say the high card is the man or woman who will portray the body?

FLORA. (*Sits in rocking chair.*) Ace high?

JASON. Of course. (*As he passes cards to* PHILIP, *then* EMILY, *and finally* FLORA. *He pulls out a card from the deck so it is obvious for* FLORA *to choose it, but she doesn't.*) This reminds me of a small experience I had while cruising the Mediterranean in a private yacht. I was posing as a North African diamond miner. Actually, I didn't have enough money to tip the stewards but somehow I got embroiled in a small game of chance with my host the last night out.

EMILY. You made enough for your tips?

JASON. My dear, in the morning, I owned the yacht. Shall we look at our cards?

EMILY. (*Turns up hers.*) Nine.

PHILIP. (*Turns up his.*) Seven.

JASON. And I believe I have the ace. (*Turns it up and it is a two.*)

FLORA. (*Rises and moves to* JASON.) I believe *I* have the ace!

JASON. But you can't. I had it in my— (*Reaches for his sleeve.*)

FLORA. They didn't call me "Fingers" for nothing. (*Hands card to* JASON.) Be sensible, Jason, you would overact and spoil the whole capon.

JASON. Very well. I concede. (*Puts cards on table and sits above table.*)

FLORA. Now for the plan. First, we have to get the mayor here. That's where you will come in, Jason. A phone call to him, beautifully put in your thrilling voice. A real chance to emote.

JASON. (*Feeling better.*) Ah. I shall rise to the occasion. But what do I say?

EMILY. (*Rises.*) That Flora fell in love with him at first sight?

FLORA. (*Crosses to* EMILY.) Emily, dear, your mind always reverts to romance.

EMILY. Force of habit. (*Sits on sofa and* FLORA *in rocking chair.*)

PHILIP. I have it! Jason, you act as Flora's adviser. Say that she is going to get a loan on her securities and save Richard but she wants to talk to the mayor first. That will get him over here fast enough.

JASON. Perfect.

EMILY. Then what happens after he gets here?

JASON. He shoots Flora.

FLORA. (*Quickly.*) With blank cartridges. I trust, Philip, you have your revolver with you?

PHILIP. (*Takes a pistol from briefcase.*) I'm never without it. Of course, since I reformed, it's full of blanks. It's always the loaded guns that go off. (*Puts pistol back in briefcase.*)

EMILY. But why does the mayor shoot dear Flora?

FLORA. It must appear an accident and then you all accuse him of murder. Cover up for him and then he'll be ready for blackmail. A reclining duck.

PHILIP. Sitting duck.

FLORA. Oh, yes. Now, Philip, you be the mayor and we'll improvise.

JASON. (*Rises.*) Improvisations are my specialty.

FLORA. But they aren't the mayor's. We want someone without ability. Philip will be perfect.

PHILIP. Now that's rather unkind.

FLORA. (*Rises and moves Center.*) I mean without acting ability. Your penmanship is without compare, Philip, but your acting is somewhat more amateur.

PHILIP. All right. I'm the mayor. (*Goes to front door.*) Clear back, everyone.

FLORA. I'll be sitting here. (*She sits on the sofa,* EMILY *fades Right.* JASON *fades to the piano.* FLORA *assumes a rather dramatically nonchalant pose on the sofa.*) Come in.

PHILIP. (*Comes in front door. He tries to imitate* RATNER *by speaking a little fast and waving his fist.*) I'm in a hurry. Haven't much time. What's the meaning of that phone call?

FLORA. Dear Mayor Ratner, I'm going to save Richard. (*She acts very dramatically.*) I'm going to borrow on my securities and help him.

PHILIP. Then I'm finished. I'll leave town. Good-bye. (*He goes out door.*)

JASON. (*Crosses to door and brings* PHILIP *back in.*) No. No. No. Come back here.

PHILIP. (*Entering.*) What's the matter?

JASON. He wouldn't act that way.

PHILIP. He wouldn't?

JASON. Here. Let me show you. (*Pushes* PHILIP *away to Left and leans against the closed door.*)

PHILIP. I had a feeling this would happen.

JASON. (*Clears his throat and assumes his act.*) Borrow on your securities? (*Crosses Down Center.*) Now, Mrs. Langley, I'm sure we can come to some agreement. Suppose I make you an offer?

FLORA. (*Holds one hand up.*) Never. A thousand times never. I can't be bought!

EMILY. (*Applauds.*) Flora, dear, you're marvelous. (PHILIP *moves to above table.*)

FLORA. (*Dropping acting pose.*) Why, thank you, Emily.

JASON. A little too dramatic perhaps.
PHILIP. The pot's calling who black?
JASON. What was that?
FLORA. Gentlemen, please. We can't afford to bicker.
JASON. (*Again the mayor.*) Mrs. Langley, you mean you'll have the money here by noon tomorrow?
FLORA. (*Dropping her character.*) Ohh, that's a good point.
JASON. I rather liked it myself.
FLORA. (*In character.*) Then you really mean to ruin Richard?
JASON. Completely.
FLORA. There is no way out. (*She picks up a nick-nack from the sofa table. Rises and holds it like a revolver.*) I shall never be able to stand the disgrace of my nephew having lost the newspaper. My life will be on your conscience. I shall kill myself. (*Holds "gun" to her heart.*)
JASON. (*Rushes to her.*) Stop. Don't! (*They struggle with the gun as he pushes her arm Upstage and then Downstage. They grunt appropriately.*)
EMILY. (*Comes in to* FLORA.) Bang!
FLORA. I am shot! You have killed me. (*She quickly lies down on the sofa.*)
PHILIP. (*Comes Center.*) Then we all rush in and say he murdered you.
JASON. He's so confused he believes it. We carry Flora outside ostensibly to bury her. Then, in the morning, we say, "Let Richard keep the paper, Mr. Mayor, or we'll tell all." (*Sits in rocking chair.*)
PHILIP. Magnificent.
FLORA. (*Sits up.*) Except for one thing.
PHILIP. What?
FLORA. Powder burns. Blank cartridges leave powder burns and a little wad comes out the barrel and it hurts. (*She pouts.*)
EMILY. (*Rushes to* FLORA.) That's true. We don't want Flora to get hurt when she's killed.
FLORA. Philip will have to fire the gun.
PHILIP. But how? From where?

FLORA. (*Crosses to* PHILIP.) The mayor and I will be struggling and you come up behind us and fire. He'll think it's the same gun. (*Pushes him towards closet.*) Get in the closet and I'll show you.

PHILIP. (*After* FLORA *pushes him in closet, closes the door, and starts back to Center, he comes out.*) How do I know when to come out?

FLORA. (*As she pushes him back in the closet again.*) When I say, "You can't stop me!"

PHILIP. (*After* FLORA *has put him in the closet and turned around to the others, he pops out again.*) I'm scared of the dark.

FLORA. (*As she again puts him in the closet.*) Pretend you're playing Blind Man's Buff. (*Crosses below the sofa.*) Over here, Jason. Now struggle with me. (*They start fighting for the gun quite slowly and methodically.*) I'm going to kill myself. It's the easiest way. Let me alone. You can't stop me! (PHILIP *comes out of the closet holding his hand like a revolver.*)

JASON. I shall stop you. I won't let you do this.

FLORA. My life is over. The disgrace is too much.

PHILIP. (*To their Left.*) Bang!

FLORA. Oooh! I am dead. Murdered! (*She teeters on the brink of death, one hand held to her heart. She takes short little steps this way and that but never quite falls down.*)

EMILY. Back in the closet, Philip, quickly.

PHILIP. Oh, yes. (*Disappears in the closet.* FLORA *continues her teetering.*)

JASON. So far so good.

FLORA. (*Stops moving.*) I haven't died yet. (*Back to her movement.*)

JASON. My dear, Bernhardt didn't take that long in CAMILLE.

FLORA. (*Decides to wait.*) I'll save myself for the real time. This should work. I'll be dead without it hurting. (*Calls.*) All right, Philip. (PHILIP *comes out.*)

EMILY. (*Sits on the sofa.*) It seems to me you're leaving an awful lot to chance.

ACT II   THE ROBIN HOOD CAPER   47

FLORA. Now for the phone call to the mayor.

JASON. (*As he goes to the phone.*) This is my moment.

EMILY. Good luck.

JASON. Thank you. (*As he picks up the phone* PHILIP *comes to his Right and* FLORA *next to* PHILIP.) Operator, I wish to speak to Mayor Ratner. I don't know the number. . . . Thank you. (*To* OTHERS.) She's getting it.

EMILY. (*Crosses to* FLORA'S *Left so they are all in a line.*) I haven't been so excited since I married a Colonel and a Brigadier General on the same day.

JASON. (*Into phone.*) Hello, Mayor Ratner. This is The Reverend Jason Bosley speaking. . . . Of course you know me. We met at Richard Collins' this afternoon. . . . Yes, that's right. It seems, Mayor, that certain matters have come to the attention of Mrs. Langley—certain financial matters. She asked me to act as her advisor and inform you that she is borrowing some money on her securities to help Richard. . . . What do you mean you don't believe me? (*To* OTHERS.) He doesn't believe me.

ALL. He must!

JASON. (*Into phone.*) You must! . . . If I were you I'd come down here right away. . . . Mrs. Langley thinks something can be worked out. . . . No, not in the morning. It's all planned for tonight. (*The* OTHERS *all "Shush" him.*) I mean, it's got to be tonight. (*Ominously.*) If you don't come, you'll be sorry. (*Hangs up.*) Idiot! He didn't believe me.

EMILY. But he's coming?

JASON. (*Sits at Left of table.*) He said so.

FLORA. This caper has got to work.

EMILY. (*Sits in rocking chair.*) Let us hope so. (PHILIP *sits above the table.*)

FLORA. If only the mayor would carry some incriminating evidence on him, I could lift it.

EMILY. I wish I could be light-fingered that way.

FLORA. (*Fades Down Center.*) It takes years of practice, dear. But it comes in handy. Once in San Francisco, I was caught by a store detective after I'd removed a very attractive emerald pin from the jewelry counter. He stopped me but I just glared at him and walked away.

EMILY. He didn't chase you?

FLORA. He couldn't. I'd taken his suspenders.

PHILIP. (*Having gotten both guns from briefcase.*) Here we are. This one is for you, Flora.

FLORA. (*Crosses to get it.*) You're sure yours is loaded with blanks?

PHILIP. Of course.

FLORA. I think I'll hide it there under that magazine. (*She indicates the movie magazine on the sofa table.*)

EMILY. A good idea.

(*The front DOORBELL rings. They* ALL *freeze for a moment.*)

JASON. To your posts! (FLORA *rushes and sits on the sofa putting the pistol on the sofa and covering it with the magazine.* JASON *and* EMILY *rush for the stairs as* PHILIP *heads for the closet with his revolver.* JASON *and* EMILY *collide, which propels* PHILIP *into the closet. Then they rush upstairs.*)

FLORA. (*Assuming her dramatic pose.*) Come in. (*The door opens and* JESSICA *is there.*)

JESS. Is Dick here, Mrs. Langley?

FLORA. Jessica! I thought you were someone else.

JESS. (*Comes Down.*) Dick was supposed to meet me at the newspaper office, but he didn't show up.

FLORA. He left a few minutes ago. You probably passed each other.

(JASON *and* EMILY *come to the landing as* JESS *crosses to below sofa.*)

JESS. He was awfully late. (*Turns to sit in rocking chair and sees the* OTHERS *on the stairs.*) Oh—hello there.

JASON. Good evening, Miss Selby.

JESS. I just came to find Dick.

EMILY. Not staying too long, are you, dear?

ACT II   THE ROBIN HOOD CAPER   49

JESS. No. I don't think so.

JASON. Good. (*He and* EMILY *go upstairs.*)

FLORA. (*As* JESS *turns to her for an explanation.*) They're very light sleepers.

JESS. (*Sits in rocking chair.*) You know you're amazing, you four. Getting together this way and devoting yourselves to charity.

FLORA. We learned the hard way. We weren't always like this, you know. People change.

JESS. You couldn't have been very much different even in Malaya. I've always wanted to go to the Far East. Tell me all about it.

FLORA. Well, Malaya is divided into two unequal parts by a range of mountains having a length of 300 miles and a breadth in places of 30 to 40 miles. The highest peak in this range, Gunong Korbu in Perak, is 7,162 feet.

JESS. I know all that. I read it in the National Geographic.

FLORA. So did I. Marvelous magazine, isn't it? But I'm much more interested in you and Richard. Tell me about the wedding plans.

JESS. That all depends on him. I wanted to set the date right now, but he's in such a mess, he won't even talk about it.

FLORA. Maybe he'll change his mind tomorrow. I have a feeling everything's going to turn out just dandy.

JESS. I don't see how.

FLORA. (*Pats the magazine under which the gun is hidden.*) Maybe you don't have as good vision as I have.

JESS. Dick's the kind of person you have to stand up to once in a while. I'm beginning to feel like Custer before his last stand. I'm about to let him have it.

FLORA. Good for you. He won't be able to answer back or he'll stutter.

JESS. (*Rises and moves in to* FLORA.) I'm going to say to him, "We're getting married and right away. You can't stop me!" (*Closet door opens.* PHILIP *quietly comes out, closes it and steps into the room holding the revolver.*) I don't care if the newspaper folds and if you're as poor as a church mouse. And what's more—" (*Turns and sees* PHILIP.) Oh, you startled me.

PHILIP. (*Points to closet door.*) I—I thought it was the bathroom.

JESS. Is that why you have a gun?

PHILIP. Oh, this. (*Laughs weakly.*) It's a water pistol. (*As he backs up the stairs.*) I wanted to fill it. In case of burglars, you know. Always keep one with me.

JESS. Wouldn't a real one be better?

PHILIP. Goodness, I'd be too scared to fire it. Well, good night. (*Rushes off.*)

FLORA. He's so kind-hearted, he won't even go hunting with a gun, always uses arrows with suction cups on the end.

DICK. (*Comes in front door.*) There you are, Jess. Weren't you supposed to meet me down at the office?

JESS. Over an hour ago.

DICK. I was a little late, I guess.

JESS. My charm seems to be diminishing. Now I'm running second to type-setting.

FLORA. (*Gives an elaborate yawn.*) My, my, but I am tired. (*Rises.*) Must be the fresh air. (*Crosses Up Center.*) You two will excuse me, I'm sure.

JESS. Of course.

DICK. Good night, Auntie. Sweet dreams. (*Kisses her.*)

FLORA. (*As she goes to the landing.*) Thank you, dear. And don't worry about your problems. They'll all vanish in the morning. There's an old saying, "Tonight's troubles are tomorrow's memories"— (*Thinks it over.*) —or something like that. (*She goes upstairs.*)

DICK. Pollyanna.

JESS. She looks on the best side of everything.

DICK. (*Moves to below table.*) I'm afraid I don't see any best side.

JESS. (*Crosses to* DICK.) Dick, my uncle wired tonight and he'll be back here tomorrow. Let's set the date right now. That'll give us something to look forward to.

DICK. Honey, we can't talk about marriage with the state everything's in.

ACT II   THE ROBIN HOOD CAPER   51

JESS. Why not?

DICK. What kind of a heel do you think I am?

JESS. Rather a nice one.

DICK. (*Moves to below rocking chair.*) You think I'd marry a girl when I'm not only out of a job, but in debt as well?

JESS. If you would have married me two months ago when you proposed, would you divorce me now just because you lost your business?

DICK. Of course not.

JESS. Then what's the difference whether I'm your wife next week or two months ago?

DICK. You women have the damnedest ways of proving a point. (*Sits in rocking chair.*)

JESS. Then why won't you marry me now?

DICK. Because I am broke!

JESS. (*Kneels by him.*) If I were your wife, I'd have to cope with it, wouldn't I? So pretend you're married to me already and we'll share this problem together.

DICK. Jessica, I—

FLORA. (*Offstage, trying to get rid of them.*) Good night, dear.

EMILY. (*Offstage. Elaborately.*) Good night, Flora.

JESS. (*Rises.*) Shh. You'll disturb them.

DICK. (*Rises.*) Just let me settle my problems for a little while and—

JASON. (*Offstage.*) Good night, Philip.

PHILIP. (*Offstage.*) Good night, Jason. Sleep well.

DICK. And then we'll set a date.

JESS. Well, that's a fine thing. Suppose another problem comes up and we postpone it again. And then another. Are you going to support me on your Social Security?

DICK. Now you're being silly.

EMILY. (*Offstage.*) Flora, dear, did you leave the radio on? I hear voices and I can't sleep.

FLORA. (*Offstage.*) No, Emily, dear, it's just Richard and Jessica. They're going to the newspaper office *right away*.

EMILY. (*Offstage.*) Oh. Good.

DICK. (*Starts for front door.*) Jess, I've got to get to the office. We'll discuss this some other time.

JESS. (*Raising her voice.*) We will discuss it now!

DICK. (*Comes back to* JESSICA.) Shh! Have some feelings for the old folks.

JESS. Dick, you either marry me now or you don't. (*Crosses to below sofa.*) I am not in the habit of chasing all the way up into the country after a man and then have to tell everyone, "No, he changed his mind."

DICK. It's better than spending your honeymoon on the welfare line.

JESS. (*Turns to* DICK.) I have some money saved up, you know that.

DICK. Now I can't support you. That's what you're saying.

JESS. That's what *you're* saying. You've been saying it all evening.

DICK. I happen to believe a man should not live off his wife. If you love me, you'll wait for me.

JESS. *If* I love you? (*Crosses to* DICK.) And when did you begin to doubt me? Maybe it's time I did some doubting. Are you trying to get out of this?

DICK. Is that what you think?

JESS. (*Crosses below* DICK *to his Left.*) It seems pretty obvious. You either set a date now or you don't.

DICK. Then I don't! I am not going to be forced into a wedding when I know it isn't the right time. I am going to say when and where we'll g-g-get mar-mar-married. (*Calms down.*) Oh, hell, now I have to lie down. (*Goes to sofa and stretches out on his stomach, his face Right.*)

JESS. I have had just about enough of this. (*Crosses above sofa and looks down on him.*) Every time we start to get anything settled, you have to lie down. Get up and finish this right now.

DICK. I c-can't. I'll st-st-stutter.

DICK. I don't care if you stutter till you sound like a motor boat. I want to get married!

DICK. (*With great control.*) It should be obvious to you that I can't discuss it any longer now. I'll get sick.

(*Rises but keeps bent over at the waist and starts for front door.*) I am going to the office, I would like you to accompany me. Either you will or you won't.

JESS. I won't.

DICK. Then I'll see you tomorrow. Good night, Jessica. (*Goes out door still bent double.*)

(JESSICA *is furious. She gives way to tears and sits in the rocking chair.* FLORA *comes down, followed by* JASON, EMILY *and* PHILIP. *They are all in night clothes.* FLORA *is in an old-fashioned nightgown and full robe,* EMILY *is similarly attired except that she wears a slumber helmet. The* MEN *are in nightgowns and bathrobes.* JASON *wears a nightcap.*)

FLORA. (*Crosses to* JESS.) We couldn't help overhearing. You were rather loud.

JESS. I'm sorry. (*Sniffling.*) We've been keeping you awake. We've never had a real fight before. He's so stubborn.

FLORA. Men are very peculiar when they're in trouble. They're quite irrational.

JESS. He certainly is.

FLORA. But tomorrow is another day.

JESS. A rotten one.

JASON. It will be a marvelous one if we can just get started.

JESS. What do you mean?

EMILY. (*Pulls her up.*) Jason means that we all need a good night's rest. In the morning, Richard will be covered with remorse and he'll be putty in your hands. I've had some experience in this sort of thing.

PHILIP. (*Sits Left of the table.*) Now you run along home and tomorrow he'll be a changed person.

JESS. I hope you're right.

EMILY. We are, dear. You'll see. (*Sits Right of the table.*)

JESS. I feel awful bringing all these problems on you when you've come up here to work on your charities.

JASON. I'm always happy considering the lilies in the field. And you, my dear girl, are a very lovely lily.

JESS. You do make me feel better somehow. (JASON *sits above the table.*) And I will come by first thing in the morning. My uncle will be here then and I'm sure he'll want to meet you four.

FLORA. (*Sits in the rocking chair.*) It will be our pleasure.

JESS. He's been my guardian ever since I lost my parents. I know you'll like him, he's the kindest soul. (*Opens front door.*)

JASON. I'm sure he is.

PHILIP. Too bad he isn't rich.

JESS. Isn't it? But he's on a pension. He retired from the force several years ago. (*The* FOUR *sit up slightly, facing front.*)

JASON. The force?

PHILIP. You *do* mean the fireman's force or the forestry force, don't you?

JESS. No—the police force.

FLORA. I was afraid of that.

JESS. In Chicago. Funny, for such a gentle man, he had a terrible nickname. Rugged Ruggles. Good night, now. (*Goes out closing the door.*)

(*The* FOUR *left on stage sit facing front in a stony silence.*)

PHILIP. (*After a long pause.*) The odds against her uncle being Rugged Ruggles are astounding!

EMILY. I don't think I want to be here in the morning.

JASON. There couldn't be two Rugged Ruggles, could there?

FLORA. Maybe we could wear masks and say we're having a ball!

EMILY. That's tomorrow's problem, dear. Tonight's is descending on us momentarily.

PHILIP. This whole caper makes me rather nervous.

ACT II   THE ROBIN HOOD CAPER   55

Don't forget to say, "You can't stop me!" and good and loud, too.

FLORA. Don't worry.

(*Front DOORBELL rings.*)

JASON. (*After a moment during which they* ALL *freeze.*) To your posts!

(PHILIP *goes into the closet,* JASON *to the stairs, and* EMILY *to* FLORA *who arranges herself on the sofa.*)

EMILY. Good luck, dear.
FLORA. Thank you, Emily.
JASON. Hurry up, this is no time for sentimentality.
EMILY. She's going to be killed and I want to wish her luck.

(BELL *rings again.*)

JASON. Hurry. (*They rush out.* FLORA *gets prepared in her position.*)

FLORA. Come in. (*The door opens and* RATNER *is there.*)

RATNER. Mrs. Langley.
FLORA. Oh, Mayor Ratner. It's you.
RATNER. (*Closes the door and comes down.*) You had the Reverend call me. You must have been expecting me.
FLORA. Yes, I was. Won't you sit down?
RATNER. I never get comfortable at a business meeting. As I understand it, you may lend Mr. Collins some money, but you wanted to see me first. What is this, some kind of squeeze-play?
FLORA. Squeeze-play?
RATNER. Come on, what do you want? A percentage? Are you trying to muscle in?
FLORA. Please speak English, Mayor Ratner. I wouldn't dream of muscling in on your racket. Oh, dear, no. You'll make a slip one day and the Feds will be on your tail. They'll throw the book at you and no mouthpiece will keep you from going up the river for twenty years. (*She*

realizes what she has said and faces front with a surprised and distressed look. RATNER *studies her closely.*)

RATNER. How do you know all that?

FLORA. I read. Now shall we be realistic?

RATNER. (*Sits in rocking chair.*) By all means. Your nephew said your money was in securities. Can you borrow on it by noon tomorrow?

FLORA. I thought you'd ask that. Not till sometime in the afternoon, but I'm sure that will be satisfactory.

RATNER. I'm afraid not. Noon tomorrow is the deadline.

FLORA. Mayor Ratner, please reconsider. (*Now really goes into her act.*) The disgrace you will bring on our name—my sister's boy losing his newspaper. Worthless and unemployed on the eve of marriage. Would you ruin two lives and make a third miserable?

RATNER. Yes. (*Rises.*) You're a sweet old lady and you know nothing of business. I've worked very hard to get where I am and I'll work harder to stay there. (*He heads for the front door.*) I think we've concluded our discussion. Good evening, Mrs. Langley.

FLORA. Wait! There is only one thing left to do. (*Pulls out revolver from under magazine. Rises.*) This!

RATNER. (*Turns.*) No, no, you wouldn't!

FLORA. Of course I would. A woman pushed into a corner is a dangerous tigress!

RATNER. (*Comes Downstage.*) Think a moment. Think what would happen if you pulled that trigger—

FLORA. Reverend Bosley has promised me eternal happiness.

RATNER. Jail. The electric chair. Don't, I beg of you. It's not worth it. Don't kill me.

FLORA. You? Oh, no, you've gotten the wrong idea entirely. I wouldn't kill *you*, Mayor. What do you think I am?

RATNER. A dangerous tigress.

FLORA. I'm going to kill myself.

RATNER. (*Greatly relieved.*) Oh, that's all right.

FLORA. It is?

RATNER. A little silly, perhaps. You'd do that just because your nephew is going to lose his newspaper?

FLORA. I'd be too unhappy to go on. (*Raises gun her heart.*)

RATNER. Well, it's your life. (*Heads for front door.*)

FLORA. Aren't you going to stop me?

RATNER. I don't see why. To each his own.

FLORA. I'm going to count to three. One. (*She looks at* RATNER *who is standing there with his face screwed up waiting for the shot.*) Two. Th-think of the scandal, Mayor.

RATNER. (*Comes down.*) What scandal?

FLORA. The shot will waken my friends. They'll come down here and find me dead and you here. This will ruin you.

RATNER. You do have a point.

FLORA. I hoped I did.

RATNER. (*Goes to her.*) Give me that revolver.

FLORA. (*Turns away from him.*) Never. You're too late.

RATNER. (*Trying to reach for it.*) Give it to me!

FLORA. You can't stop me. (*She turns and they* BOTH *have hold of the revolver. She overprojects towards the closet door.*) I said, "You can't stop me!" (*Closet door opens and* PHILIP *comes out with his revolver.*)

RATNER. Now don't be a silly old fool.

FLORA. Now you've gone too far. I'm going to die now.

RATNER. I'll get that thing away from you. You can't ruin me. (PHILIP *fires the revolver close to them, then darts back to the closet door.* FLORA *screams and goes into her teetering death scene.* EMILY *and* JASON *rush down the stairs.*)

JASON. Flora, what is it?

EMILY. I heard a shot.

FLORA. I—I—

RATNER. She shot herself. I tried to stop her.

JASON. (*Pushes* RATNER *aside and goes to* FLORA.) Flora, lie down here. Let me help you. (EMILY *goes to the right of the sofa and they help* FLORA *to lie down.*)

PHILIP. Ratner, you murderer.

RATNER. But I was trying to stop her.

PHILIP. A likely story. (*Pushes* RATNER *Left and goes beside* JASON.)

EMILY. Flora, dear, does it hurt much?

FLORA. Only when I talk.

RATNER. Then shut up!

EMILY. (*Kneels by the sofa in tears.*) My dearest friend!

JASON. What happened? (PHILIP *goes to above sofa and* JASON *kneels to the Left of* FLORA.)

FLORA. I was pleading for Richard and then Mayor Ratner— (*Points at him.*) him! He—he—it's his fault.

RATNER. It's a lie. A damned lie.

PHILIP. (*To* RATNER.) Don't shout. (*Whispers.*) Can't you let her last few minutes be peaceful?

RATNER. (*Whispers.*) It's a damned lie.

EMILY. Flora, speak to me. (PHILIP *returns to above sofa.*)

FLORA. Emily, dear, is that you?

EMILY. Yes, Flora.

FLORA. Turn on the lights.

EMILY. But they *are* on. (EMILY *gasps and looks to the* OTHERS.)

FLORA. Oh, it's getting so dark.

PHILIP. She's going fast.

FLORA. One last request.

JASON. Anything.

FLORA. Bury me out there. In the sweet earth of the country—in the arms of Mother Nature.

EMILY. As you wish.

FLORA. And, Mayor Ratner, I forgive you. We all forgive him, don't we?

ALL. Yes.

FLORA. Good-bye, dear friends. (*Sinks back on sofa.*)

JASON. She's gone.   EMILY. Flora.

(*They* ALL *bow their heads, including* RATNER.)

ACT II   THE ROBIN HOOD CAPER

FLORA. (*Rises up again after a moment.*) Charles Dickens knew what he was talking about. It *is* a far, far better rest I go to than I have ever known. (*Sinks back.*)

RATNER. She's not—not—?

PHILIP. (*Takes her pulse.*) Yes, she is!

RATNER. But I didn't mean it.

PHILIP. She forgave you. We all forgave you.

JASON. I am moved to say a few words.

EMILY. (*To remind* JASON *to get* FLORA *out of there. Rises dramatically and goes to French windows.*) Not here. Out there—out there where she wants to be.

PHILIP. (*To Right of sofa.*) Yes, let us take her out to Mother Nature.

RATNER. What have I done? It all happened so quickly.

JASON. (*Crosses to* RATNER.) My son, you leave this to us, her best friends. Come back in the morning and we'll talk then. (*Puts his hands on* RATNER's *shoulders and forces him to kneel.*) Not now. Our hearts are too heavy.

RATNER. Forgive me. Oh, forgive me. (*Bows his head.*)

JASON. We'll see. Come, Philip, help me. (*Since* RATNER *has his head bowed,* FLORA *stands up and* JASON *takes her by the shoulders and* PHILIP *by the feet.* EMILY *runs and opens the front door.* EMILY *gives a musical note and they start singing as they slowly take* FLORA *to the front door.*)

      Rock of Ages
      Cleft for me,
      Let me hide myself in thee.
      While I draw this fleeting breath,
      When my eyelids close in death—

(FLORA *sneezes.* RATNER *looks up at them. The* OTHERS *freeze in panic.* PHILIP *says "Gesundheit, Emily!"* EMILY *says "Thank you." Looks at* RATNER *who again bows his head. They rush* FLORA *off.*)

      When I soar to worlds unknown,
      See thee on thy judgement throne . . .

(RATNER *is still kneeling as:*)

The CURTAIN falls

ACT THREE

TIME: *Next morning.*

AT RISE: *A very nervous* HUBERT RATNER *is pacing the room. The French windows and front door are open. He is wearing a subdued suit. After a moment, he glances up the stairs, puts out his cigarette at telephone table and talks into the phone.*

RATNER. 607. . . . Warren? Ratner here. Listen . . . I know it's early. (*Sarcastically.*) I'm sorry if I woke you but there's trouble. I won't be in the office till later. . . . No, I can't go into it over the phone. . . . Yes, by all means take your tranquilizer and then hurry down there and wait for me . . . very important, but I think I can handle it.

EMILY. (*Offstage upstairs.*) I'll be down in a minute, Philip.

RATNER. I gotta hang up now. (*Does so and crosses to the window.* PHILIP *slowly comes downstairs. He is dressed in a black suit and black tie. He has a black-edged handkerchief in his breast pocket.*) Good morning, Mr. Mullins. The door was open—

PHILIP. It's hardly a *good* morning, is it? (*Pulls out handkerchief and dabs at his nose, crosses to the sofa and sits dejectedly.*)

(JASON *comes down the stairs. He is also dressed all in black. He speaks from the landing.*)

JASON. My son, though our heart is heavy, I am sure yours is heavier.

RATNER. I'm sure we—

JASON. (*Holds up his hand.*) Please. I am meditating. (*He sits in the rocking chair. After a moment,* EMILY *comes to the landing and collapses against the wall in tears. She is dressed in deep mourning, including a black veil over her face. She cries into a large, black handkerchief.*)

PHILIP. Please, Emily, don't. You must be brave.

EMILY. I'll try. (*She sits Right of table. After a pause, she suddenly bursts into fresh tears.*) I'm sorry. Please forgive me.

JASON. Mayor Ratner.

RATNER. Yes.

JASON. It seems we shall have to shed our veil of woe and discuss facts. Emily, please try to control yourself.

EMILY. I'm trying. Really, I am. (*But she bursts into new tears.* RATNER, *exasperated, moves above the sofa to the window.* FLORA, *unable to contain herself, peeks down the stairs. She is in a daytime cotton dress.*) Flora was so good and so kind. To think I'll never see her sweet little face again—her smile, her twinkling eyes.

PHILIP. She was one in a million. A true friend. (*The* THREE *nod.* FLORA *nods after them.*) Her joy in life was to give, to help others.

JASON. Heaven is brighter this morning for a new angel being in it.

EMILY. I shall carry the beauty of Flora's ideals with me always. But I shall never be happy again. (*She weeps again. The* OTHERS, *except for* RATNER, *brush tears from their eyes.* FLORA *gives a gasp of regret and runs upstairs.* JASON *and* PHILIP *see her,* RATNER *faces front listening and* EMILY *weeps.*)

RATNER. Did you hear something?

JASON. Maybe it's raining— (RATNER *glances out French windows and then looks back at* JASON.)

EMILY. Flora has not given her life in vain. She must rank with Edith Cavell, Joan of Arc, Madame Pompadour.

PHILIP. Did she give her life?

EMILY. She must have. She'd be over two hundred years old by now.

JASON. Flora did not give her life in vain, Emily. Mayor Ratner will see to that.

RATNER. I will?

JASON. Of course. Flora's biggest worry was the happiness of her nephew. How can we expect her to rest peacefully unless we have helped him to reach his desires? Mayor Ratner, I know you will gladly hand Richard the deed to the newspaper office.

RATNER. I will what?

JASON. To make our beloved Flora happy.

RATNER. (*Furious, he crosses Center.*) Now you're being ridiculous. I didn't kill her, why should I care if she's happy?

PHILIP. A shocking statement.

JASON. If necessary, we three will have to testify that her dying statement was, "Mayor Ratner shot me."

RATNER. But you know it was an accident. You said so last night.

JASON. We've thought it over and we're not so sure.

EMILY. Not sure at all.

RATNER. What's going on here?

PHILIP. We're just trying to make Flora happy.

RATNER. You all think you're pretty clever, don't you?

JASON. Sir?

RATNER. Well, it so happens I am mayor here and I have some authority. You realize all I have to do is to have you locked up for a few hours, dig up the body, and you won't be able to prove a thing?

JASON. That's true, isn't it?

PHILIP. Oh, dear, he does have the best of us.

RATNER. I'm glad you realize that.

EMILY. Except, Mayor Ratner, you don't know where the body is buried.

RATNER. (*After a pause.*) Well—it's— (*Crosses to French windows.*) out there—somewhere.

EMILY. Um-hmm, somewhere. I can't remember exactly where. Can you, Philip?

PHILIP. Nooo, I can't. How about you, Jason?

JASON. It seems to have slipped my mind, but I'm sure I can remember when I want to.

PHILIP. When do you think you'll want to?

ACT III   THE ROBIN HOOD CAPER   63

JASON. Oh, maybe tomorrow, maybe the next day, or maybe even the day before Election Day.

RATNER. (*As they all stare at him.*) Of course you know where it is. You buried it.

JASON. When you get to be our age, the memory slips a bit. Now, about that deed to the newspaper office . . .

RATNER. You know what this is?

EMILY. I believe it's called bluemail.

PHILIP. Black, dear. Blackmail.

JASON. The time is getting on towards noon. I should think if you hurried, Mayor, you could be back in quite short order.

RATNER. But I—

JASON. (*Rises.*) I believe we left our shovels in the garage, didn't we, Philip?

PHILIP. (*Rises.*) I believe we did. Shall we change before we start digging?

RATNER. No, no. (*Crosses to Center.*) I'll get the deed. (BOTH MEN *sit.*)

EMILY. A very wise move.

RATNER. But I'll also want a signed statement from you that this whole thing was an accident.

JASON. Of course . . . Don't you trust us?

RATNER. I don't know. You look like sweet, normal old people, but—

EMILY. That's all we are. Just old people trying to put a silver lining into the dark cloud of the late Flora Langley.

PHILIP. You'd better hurry.

RATNER. But you stay here. Don't do any "gardening" till I get back. (*He rushes out the front door.*)

JASON. (*Looks out the door after him.*) He's rushing off as if the devil were after him. (*Closes the door.*)

EMILY. Then I can take this onion out of my handkerchief now. (*Takes half an onion out of her handkerchief and removes the veil from her head and places it on the table.*)

PHILIP. Our caper is certainly running on schedule so far.

FLORA. (*Rushes downstairs.*) My dears, you were magnificent. I was so carried away, I had to put Murine in my eyes. I never knew I would be missed so much.

EMILY. I can't stop crying. It's this onion.

FLORA. I'll put it back in the vegetable bin. (*Exits into kitchen.* JASON *sits in the chair above the table.*)

PHILIP. After we get the deed, we'd better slip quietly out of town. Our meeting will be cut short, but think of the good we have done. A new zenith for Charities Anonymous.

EMILY. But we mustn't forget to solve the romantic problem. Richard and Jessica seemed far from lovebirds last night.

FLORA. (*Re-enters.*) I think I'll send her a fur coat for a wedding present. Do you think she'd like sheared beaver? It's in this season. There's a hospital bridge next month and I usually get my choice of coats there. (*Sits chair Left of table.*) I must get Jessica's size.

PHILIP. Also, we must get the mayor to resign from his re-election campaign.

JASON. Philip, why don't you draft the article of resignation?

PHILIP. I'd be honored. For the occasion, I think I'll do it in Dwight D. Eisenhower's handwriting.

EMILY. I tried to marry Eisenhower once. Maybe I should have worn bangs.

DICK. (*Comes down from upstairs. He is putting on a sports jacket.*) Good morning. Have you all had breakfast?

FLORA. Ages ago, thank you.

DICK. Sleep well?

JASON. We had a lot of work to do, but we did manage a few winks.

DICK. Good. Jess didn't call, did she?

FLORA. No.

DICK. (*Disappointed, crosses to window.*) Oh.

EMILY. Were you expecting her to?

DICK. I thought she might.

EMILY. (*Crosses to* DICK.) In *l'affaires de coeur*, I am a specialist. I detect a little lover's spat, don't I?

DICK. There's no sense in worrying you.

EMILY. Maybe we can help.

DICK. (*Turns away.*) It's just that I won't get married with things in such a state. That's all.

EMILY. Then your problem is over. (*Sits in rocking chair.*) There. Wasn't that simple?

DICK. What do you mean?

FLORA. Emily means that we had a little chat with the mayor and he's not going to throw you out.

DICK. When did you talk to Ratner?

FLORA. This morning. I'm not very good at explaining business matters, but Jason, with his keen human insight, made the mayor see he was misbehaving. We even think he may not campaign for re-election.

EMILY. And so you and Jessica can set the date. Romance always triumphs.

DICK. (*Crosses to French windows.*) Now come on, no one can put anything over on Ratner. He doesn't have changes of heart.

FLORA. Nevertheless he has.

JASON. Never underestimate the goodness of your fellow man. All sinners repent.

PHILIP. Amen.

DICK. Did you give him some money?

FLORA. (*Rises and moves Up Center.*) You know our money is tied up. We just persuaded him. Now, don't think any more about it. He's coming back with the deed and give it to you.

DICK. Something funny's going on here.

(*Front DOORBELL rings.*)

JASON. It's the Mayor!

PHILIP. Flora—run! (FLORA *flees for the stairs as fast as she can, which is not fast at all.* DICK *goes to the front door.*)

JASON. (*To* DICK.) Perhaps we should talk to him privately.

DICK. (*Opens door.*) Jessica. (JESSICA *comes in dressed in a nice dress.*)

FLORA. (*Caught on the landing.*) Thank goodness. (*Comes downstairs again.*)

JESS. I'm coming in whether you ask me to or not.

DICK. Why wouldn't I ask you in?

JESS. I don't know what mood you're in this morning. You're so changeable. (*To the* OTHERS *cheerily.*) Good morning. (*They exchange greetings with her.*)

FLORA. (*Moves to above rocking chair. Tries to usher the* OTHERS *out.*) Come along, everyone. Let's go upstairs. I'm sure Jessica and Richard want to be alone. They have such a lot to talk about.

JESS. Maybe we do and maybe we don't. It depends on your pig-headed nephew.

DICK. You're the one who's pig-headed.

PHILIP. (*Crosses to stairs.*) If you'll excuse me, I have to do some important handwriting upstairs.

EMILY. Huh?

PHILIP. Dwight D. Eisenhower.

EMILY. Oh, yes, and I have to help him. (*She rises.*)

JASON. (*Rises.*) Me, too. Enjoy yourselves, my children, and remember marriages are made in Heaven. (*They go upstairs with* FLORA *shooing them ahead of her.*)

FLORA. (*To* JESS.) You look radiant this morning, dear. Love brings beauty to a woman.

JESS. I feel like a hag. I had an awful time getting to sleep. Then I kept having funny dreams. I must have dreamt of a wedding. I could hear hymns being sung—clear as day—"Rock of Ages."

FLORA. (*Worried.*) How comforting. I always dream of Rock 'n' Roll. (*Starts up the stairs.*)

JESS. (*Stopping her on the landing.*) You don't look so well, though. Didn't you sleep?

FLORA. Oh, yes, wonderfully, my dear. If I look dead,

well—I'm a better actress than I thought I was. (*Exits upstairs.*)

DICK. You seem in a rather belligerent mood.

JESS. (*Bangs her purse down on the table.*) How else do you expect me to feel after being turned down last night? Hell hath no fury and so forth.

DICK. I didn't turn you down. I postponed you.

JESS. I'm like Christmas. I can't be postponed. Ready or not, I'm here. (*Crosses down.*) My uncle came this morning and I've got him waiting outside. He wants to know the date of our wedding and so do I. What shall I say?

DICK. (*Comes down.*) I haven't changed my mind since last night. We'll get married when I am solvent enough to afford you. (*Thinks it over.*) Which may be in a few minutes.

JESS. What do you mean? Oh, darling, something's happened, hasn't it?

DICK. I don't know. My guests claim they talked to the mayor and somehow everything has been settled in my favor. I don't believe it, but you never can tell.

JESS. What did they do?

DICK. (*Moves below sofa.*) They're very vague about it but they seem so convinced.

JESS. Hallelujah! I'll live on that hope for the rest of the morning. (*Crosses to* DICK.) If you still have the paper, then when will the wedding be?

DICK. (*Sits on the sofa.*) You have a one track mind.

JESS. Definitely. (*Sits beside him.*) How about a week from Saturday? You can always get a better crowd on weekends.

DICK. Jessica, if I have the newspaper a week from Saturday, I'll gladly marry you.

JESS. I'll go tell Uncle. (*Starts to leave.*)

DICK. *If,* remember!

JESS. I can't start asking people to a tentative wedding. We'll get married anyway.

DICK. We will not.

JESS. Now don't start that again.

DICK. I never stopped it.

JESS. You can't say you'll marry me one minute and then take back the offer the next. That's breach of promise.

DICK. All right, then don't make it a week from Saturday. (*Crosses to French windows.*) There! Now that's safe. That's settled.

JESS. No, it isn't. I didn't hear you. You said a week from Saturday and I'm going to tell my uncle and I'm going to invite everyone and if you don't want to show up, you don't have to. We'll have a wake or a wedding. It's up to you.

DICK. You can't force a man into a wedding.

JESS. Why not? Every other woman does.

DICK. (*Crosses to* JESSICA.) I won't be railroaded into this.

JESS. You can't help it.

DICK. I'll refuse to show up.

JESS. Then everyone will feel sorry for me and hate you.

DICK. It's time someone really took hold of you.

JESS. (*Moves right up to him.*) Go ahead, then.

DICK. You are the most stubborn, willful woman I have ever known. (*Gets good and mad.*) I will marry you when I am good and ready and not one minute before. *I* will set the date and *I* will set the time and the pl pl-place. And no arrogant, sel-sel-selfish wom-wom-woman . . . oh, hell.

JESS. (*Starts to help him to sofa.*) You'd better lie down.

DICK. (*Furious.*) I will not lie down. No arrogant, sel-selfish woman . . .

JESS. You'll get sick.

DICK. This is too important. Sel-selfish woman is going to hood-hoodwink me . . .

JESS. Be calm, Dick.

DICK. (*Really taking the roof off the place.*) Don't tell me to be calm! I have been calm all my life and it hasn't done me a damned bit of good!

JESS. You're not stuttering.
DICK. I'm not, am I?
JESS. Go on. Go on, darling, keep getting mad. You're breaking through.
DICK. I am? (*Thinks it over.*) I am!
JESS. Yell. Hurl invectives at me. Keep it up!
DICK. You fiend! You low, conniving rat!
JESS. (*Jumping up and down and laughing happily.*) That's it, darling! That's it!
DICK. (*Happily yelling.*) You stinker! You rotten, dirty louse!
JESS. You're getting over it. You're curing yourself. Keep it up.

(FLORA *comes down the stairs followed by* EMILY, JASON, *and* PHILIP *in that order. They have heard the screaming and are mystified.*)

DICK. You contemptible rotter! You slimy, disgusting creature!
FLORA. (*Comes between them.*) Richard, dear—please!
DICK. (*Pushes* FLORA *to the Right,* EMILY *rushes to her.*) You scheming hypocrite! You lying cheat!
JASON. (*At his Left.*) My son, really.
EMILY. You'll regret this.
PHILIP. (*By Left of table.*) Stop, in the name of decency.
DICK. You Jezebel. You Medusa. You Borgia.
JESS. Oh, Aunt Flora, he loves me. He loves me. (*Throws her arms around him and they kiss.*)
FLORA. This modern love-making escapes me.
EMILY. (*To sofa Right.*) I never got a man that way.
JASON. Most unusual.
DICK. I did it!
JESS. You sure did. Oh, Dick, you did it for me. You broke through your sound barrier.
PHILIP. He was loud enough, if that's what you mean.
JESS. Nothing can stop you now. You can tell everyone off without getting sick.

DICK. You bet I can. Just watch out.

JESS. I'll be right back. I've got to spread the news about the date. (*Runs out front door. She leaves the door open.* EMILY *sits on the sofa.*)

FLORA. Richard, dear, does this mean you've set the wedding day?

DICK. (*In a daze.*) I guess so. A week from Saturday come hell or high water. Excuse me, Reverend.

JASON. I often use the word myself. (*Sits Right of table.*)

DICK. I broke through, Aunt Flora. Jess told me to calm down and I broke through. I didn't stutter. I didn't have to lie down. I'm cured!

FLORA. I guess when we want something badly enough, it makes all the difference. (*Sits in rocking chair.*)

DICK. It sure does. Now if only I can keep the newspaper.

FLORA. Don't worry, dear. It's all being taken care of. (*Gets her work out.*)

JASON. When the mayor returns, you'll see.

PHILIP. But be sure and leave us alone to iron out the arrangements.

DICK. This all seems quite illegal to me.

EMILY. Nonsense. (*Picks up magazine from sofa table.*)

PHILIP. This specially prepared document will make it all legal. (*Pulls paper out of suit pocket.*)

DICK. I don't understand any of this.

FLORA. You're not supposed to.

(JESS *runs in dragging her uncle behind her.* FREDERICK RUGGLES *is a pleasant looking middle-aged man who shows great strength. His gruffness hides quite a warm heart.*)

JESS. Here's Uncle, and he gives his consent.

(*The* FOUR OLDER PEOPLE *disappear immediately.* FLORA *puts her work up in front of her face,* EMILY *hides behind the magazine,* JASON *picks a magazine off the table and hides behind it. It is one of the Confession magazines.* PHILIP *pulls his handkerchief from his breast pocket and covers his face with it.*)

DICK. (*As he shakes hands with* FREDERICK.) Nice to see you again, sir.

FREDERICK. I'm delighted about this, my boy. Delighted. I'm sure you'll both be very happy.

DICK. Thank you. And now I want you to meet some very good friends of mine. (*He turns and sees his guests all hidden. Tries to carry off the situation.*) This is my aunt, Mrs. Langley. (FREDERICK *comes down and extends his hand to* FLORA.)

FREDERICK. Pleased to meet you, Mrs. Langley.

FLORA. (*Her hand comes out from behind her work.*) How do?

DICK. And Mrs. Jordan.

EMILY. (*From behind magazine.*) Charmed.

DICK. The Reverend Bosley.

JASON. (*As* FREDERICK *moves to him.*) My son.

DICK. (*Completely confused.*) And Philip Mullins.

FREDERICK. Very glad to meet you. (PHILIP *gives a small grunt from behind his handkerchief.*)

DICK. Auntie, would you mind not sewing right now?

FLORA. I'm almost finished. (*With a look and double meaning to* EMILY.) I can't put it down now!

JESS. (*To* FREDERICK.) They're really awfully sweet as a rule.

FREDERICK. (*Looking at them.*) Langley, Jordan, Reverend Bosley, and Mullins. This sounds familiar.

JASON. Oh—oh.

FREDERICK. (*Loud.*) Look at me. (*There is a pause while they freeze.*) Look at me! (*The* FOUR *slowly lower their work and look at him with a faint, sweet smile.*) What is this—another Appalachian meeting?

DICK. What do you mean?

FREDERICK. Jessica, what sort of people are you associating with?

JESS. What's the matter, Uncle?

FREDERICK. Perhaps you don't know them as well as I do.

DICK. You've met my guests before?

FREDERICK. Your guests? I met them when they were guests of the state of Illinois. They weren't names, they were numbers!

DICK. Numbers?

FREDERICK. Come on, Richard, surely you know your aunt, if that's what she is, was known as Fingers Langley?

DICK. Fingers?

FREDERICK. (*As* JESS *moves to behind* FLORA.) And what about Emily Jordan? (*Crosses to* EMILY.) Still using that name, huh? When I knew her, she was Mrs. Emily Jordan Johnson Creighton Brown Culver Rothchild Maloney. And that was before we really started checking her marital record.

EMILY. Some women like hats—I like husbands. (JESS *crosses to above* EMILY.)

FREDERICK. (*Crosses to* JASON.) And here we have The Chameleon. Old Bosley, a reverend now.

JASON. I don't claim to be a minister. I like to wear my collar backwards and everyone just assumes.

FREDERICK. (*Crosses above table*.) And Mullins, the best forger in the business. He could even chip the Rosetta Stone out of putty from memory.

PHILIP. Praise from Caesar!

DICK. Wait a minute, Mr. Ruggles—

FLORA. Richard, dear, he's known as Rugged Ruggles.

JESS. (*Sits Right of* EMILY *on the sofa*.) It's a small world.

FREDERICK. (*To* FLORA.) I see you haven't forgotten.

FLORA. (*Puts her sewing in the bag*.) It seems it's time for a long over-due explanation.

DICK. I should think so. Fingers, husbands, Rosetta Stones. (*Moves above table*.) What's it all mean?

FLORA. And, Jessica, you should know the skeleton in the Collins closet if you're going to marry Richard. It seems what Mr. Ruggles has said is perfectly true. (*Rises and moves to* RICHARD.) When you were a small child, Richard, I ran afoul of the law and instead of going to Malaya as I led you to believe, I went to a charming little prison. (DICK *sits above the table.*) Your mother thought the Malaya story was the best thing all round. She thought having an aunt in jail might warp your personality. Well, anyway, my debt to society has been taken care of along with these other three, and I'd just as soon nothing was ever mentioned of this distressing time in our lives again.

DICK. I don't believe it. You four are crooks?

FLORA. We detest the word. (*Crosses above sofa.*) We paid, and our conscience is clear. Who are you three to cast a stone at us? We paid and you didn't. I bet, in a way, you're all guilty, too.

DICK. Guilty of what?

FLORA. (*Moves towards* DICK.) Richard, did you ever find a penny in the street?

DICK. I guess so.

FLORA. And you picked it up and never reported it?

DICK. Sure—why not?

FLORA. That's a crime. If it was ten thousand dollars, would you have reported it?

DICK. Of course.

FLORA. Where do you draw the line? At one dollar? At a thousand? Where? You're guilty! (*Crosses above sofa towards* JESS.) And you, Jessica, have you ever checked out at the supermarket and watched them undercharge you for something?

JESS. They usually overcharge, but sometimes, I suppose—

FLORA. Guilty! And Rugged Ruggles, how about you? (*Crosses Center.*) Did you ever make a phone call and after you hung up, have the dime come back and kept it?

FREDERICK. Who hasn't?

FLORA, EMILY, JASON, PHILIP. (*All together.*) Guilty!

FLORA. There. You're all morally guilty and you never paid for your crimes. We did. You should ask our forgiveness.

FREDERICK. (*Crosses below* FLORA *to the window.*) There's something wrong with this line of reasoning.

FLORA. Ever since we met at the parole office, we've been as good as gold. It's all your doing, Mr. Ruggles. You persuaded us to go straight. We're shining examples of your technique in dealing with the repentant criminal. (*Crosses to* FREDERICK.) We banded together and formed a Charities Anonymous Club. We have devoted ourselves to good works. (*Crosses to rocking chair.*) I admit sometimes we have to step a teensy little bit over the line to accomplish our ends but it's always for the other fellow. And now you come charging in here making out as if we were all lepers or something. (*She starts to cry and sits in the rocking chair.*) I don't think it's fair.

FREDERICK. (*Moves down to above the sofa.*) Now, Mrs. Langley, I know you're all square with society. But what's this charity business?

FLORA. Philip, there, has saved thousands of lives with his new wing on the hospital. Children will walk again because Emily contributed so much to polio. We've all done magnificent things unselfishly, nobly, and now you come along and spoil everything.

JASON. Just when we're right in the midst of one of our greatest projects. We're saving an entire town and you'd better not ruin it.

DICK. (*Rises.*) Are you getting me back the newspaper dishonestly?

FLORA. Don't quibble.

DICK. (*Crosses Center.*) I want to know.

PHILIP. Just let us talk to the mayor. That's all we ask. Trust us.

EMILY. Jessica, don't let your uncle spoil it.

FREDERICK. (*Crosses to* DICK.) Well, this town is outside my jurisdiction and I am retired, but still—

EMILY. (*To* JESS.) Please.

JESS. Uncle, come along, let me give you a cup of coffee. (*Crosses to* FREDERICK *and pulls him by the hand to the kitchen.*)

FREDERICK. But I—

JESS. Later, Uncle.
FREDERICK. (*As they disappear into the kitchen.*) I might have uncovered another Murder Incorporated!
DICK. Auntie, I can't believe it. You in jail?
FLORA. Don't dwell on it. Just erase it from your mind.
DICK. All of you—ex-cons!
JASON. We prefer to think we went away for a cure. (*Exasperated*, DICK *crosses away Left.*)
EMILY. The good we've done will live after us, the evil will be forgotten.
RATNER. (*From Offstage.*) Here's the deed to the newspaper office!

(*They are galvanized into action.* FLORA *hits the floor below the sofa.* EMILY *rises and steps between her and Center. She holds her skirt open wide to conceal* FLORA. *The* OTHERS *rise.*)

JASON. (*As* RATNER *enters waving the bank deed.*) That was nice and fast. Let me see it?
RATNER. I am not through yet, Mr. Collins. I shall get even with you for this flagrant bit of blackmail.
DICK. Blackmail?
RATNER. What else do you call it? (*Pulls a typed sheet of paper from his pocket.*) I have here a paper for the three of you to sign which completely exonerates me.
DICK. From what?
RATNER. I want it signed before I hand over this deed.
DICK. I don't understand this at all. Aunt Flora, perhaps you had better explain— (*Looks around* RATNER *for* FLORA *but she is not there.*) Aunt Flora. Where is she?
EMILY. Shh!
JASON. Not now, Richard.
PHILIP. Quiet!
DICK. (*Sees* FLORA *behind* EMILY. *Crosses to her.*) Auntie, what's the matter? She's fainted.
FLORA. (*Waving him away.*) Go away!
DICK. Someone help me.
RATNER. (*Crosses to* FLORA. DICK *is helping her up.*

RATNER *starts to help him.*) Mrs. Langley, but—what the hell is going on? She's not dead!

DICK. Of course not.

RATNER. But last night—oh, now I get it. (*Crosses Center.*) Think you're all pretty clever, don't you? The oldest trick in the business. You can get up, Mrs. Langley, it's all over. You poor, conniving amateurs.

FLORA. Amateurs? We fooled you last night.

RATNER. This is this morning. Now, let me make myself clear. This deed (*Taps his pocket.*) is going back to the bank until noon when I shall throw you out of town, Mr. Collins, and bring charges against them for extortion unless they go with you.

FLORA. We tried, Richard.

DICK. I don't know what you did but I thank you for trying.

FREDERICK. (*As he comes in followed by* JESS.) It's highly unusual, Jess, but—well, that does it! (*Pointing at* RATNER.) You can't tell me he's turned straight, too.

JESS. Who?

FREDERICK. Him! Hubie, the Heist!

DICK. Hubie the what?

FREDERICK. Heist!

RATNER. Ruggles, where did you come from?

JESS. Uncle, this is Mayor Ratner.

FREDERICK. Mayor? Ha! He's Hubie the Heist. He'd steal the pennies off his own mother's eyes. He has a record as long as Dillinger's.

DICK. Our "honest" mayor?

FREDERICK. And what charity is he supporting?

FLORA. No, he's not one of us. Far from it—he's a very bad man.

DICK. Our Mayor with a record. (*Crosses to* RATNER.) Well, won't that make good copy for my newspaper, or any newspaper for that matter, in case mine isn't operating past noon today.

RATNER. I think it will be. (*Crosses to* FREDERICK.) Now, Ruggles, don't get excited. I haven't been doing anything I shouldn't.

ACT III THE ROBIN HOOD CAPER 77

DICK. Graft isn't something you shouldn't?

FREDERICK. I'll just drop in at the local police station and have them check on you.

PHILIP. He runs the police department.

FREDERICK. Then I'll go to the county seat.

DICK. (*Crosses Up Right of the table.*) I think our Mayor will be leaving town before they can investigate.

PHILIP. I have a small slip of paper here saying that you are not campaigning for re-election, Mr. Mayor. (RATNER *takes it.*) I guess it's unnecessary now.

RATNER. I guess it is. Anyway, it's already signed Dwight D. Eisenhower. (*Hands it back to* PHILIP.)

PHILIP. I got carried away.

(WARREN *comes in the front door followed by his wife,* SYLVIA. SYLVIA COATES *is a middle-aged, attractive matron a little socially conscious of her position.*)

WARREN. (*Comes Center.*) There you are, Hubert. Something fishy's going on in this town and I don't like it. All the parking meters are empty.

(FLORA, JASON, *and* PHILIP *turn to* EMILY *who looks sheepish.*)

EMILY. I got up early. (*Sits.*)

WARREN. And at seven this morning, my wife here found a bundle of thirty-seven hundred dimes on the front porch.

SYLVIA. It was addressed to me as President of the Mothers March for Polio.

WARREN. Is there some connection?

RATNER. (*Crosses to* WARREN.) Shut up, Warren. There are more important things to be considered. I have just decided to resign as Mayor of Bridgeway Corners.

WARREN. Resign? Why?

RATNER. This is Frederick Ruggles, formerly of the Chicago Police Department.

WARREN. Yipe!

RATNER. And the others act like recreation hour at Sing-Sing. I'll send you a postcard from somewhere, Warren. Maybe we can set up shop in Pago-Pago. (*He rushes quickly out the front door, leaving it open.*)

SYLVIA. Warren, do you mean this policeman is investigating Hubert?

WARREN. Hubert has a past, my dear.

SYLVIA. Heavens, the Woman's Club just elected him most likely to succeed to a fifth term.

WARREN. Then you'd better have them change the vote to me. I shall take over where Hubert left off.

DICK. Out of the frying pan into the fire. (JESS *crosses to him.* JASON *and* PHILIP *sit.*)

FLORA. Mr. Ruggles, you don't happen to recognize this gentleman, do you?

FREDERICK. I'm afraid not.

FLORA. Too bad. (*She sits.*)

WARREN. How's it sound, Sylvia? Mayor Warren Coates.

SYLVIA. Oh—me, the mayor's wife? Hubert always had you too much under his thumb, dear. Now you can expand. (*Moves down and directs line to* FLORA.) I must send this in to my home-town newspaper. They always thought little Sylvia Spring wouldn't amount to anything.

JASON. Spring? Your name was Spring?

SYLVIA. Yes. I always say that's why I'll never divorce Warren. Then my name would be Spring Coates. Silly, isn't it?

JASON. (*Rises.*) Spring Coates! (*Laughs.*) Of course, that's why you look familiar. Let's see, it must be about thirty years ago in a small town in Arizona. Yuma, wasn't it? I lived at 38 Cactus Drive that winter.

SYLVIA. Cactus Drive? Of course, you're the Reverend Bosley. You married us!

JASON. In a manner of speaking. Of course it was an unusual ceremony. I believe I was using a French dictionary for a prop at the time.

SYLVIA. Isn't that the funniest thing, Warren?

ACT III THE ROBIN HOOD CAPER 79

WARREN. Sylvia! As usual, you're not paying attention. He is not a minister. He is a fake. (JASON *sits*.)

SYLVIA. (*To* WARREN.) Warren, what does this mean?

WARREN. It means you've opened your mouth once too often. We're not married.

SYLVIA. But, Warren, our little boy—our little Judson —then he's a—

FLORA. Please, Mrs. Coates.

DICK. Well, this is quite a morning. Are you going to campaign for mayor with a common-law wife by your side?

WARREN. Come along, my dear, we'd best start packing. (*Starts to lead her to door*.)

SYLVIA. (*Breaks away from him*.) This is hardly the time to take me on vacation.

WARREN. (*With a smile*.) As a matter of fact, I don't have to take you anywhere. (*He sits her in the rocking chair*.) I'll mail you a post card from Pago-Pago. (*He runs out after giving the chair a push so that* SYLVIA *is left rocking and perplexed*.)

SYLVIA. I really don't understand any of this. (*Rises and heads for door. Turns*.) Nice to met you all, I think. (*Runs out*.) Warren, wait for me. You need me. The car is in my name!

DICK. (*Crosses Center*.) I don't really understand any of this either, but I assume I'm running for mayor unopposed, that I have the newspaper back, and that I'm going to get married a week from Saturday.

JESS. (*Crosses to* DICK.) You see, darling, everything worked out for the best.

DICK. I'm going to put out an edition of *The Clarion* that'll knock this town on its ear. Come on. (*Starts to take her out*.)

JESS. (*Stops him*.) Dick. The deed. We never got it from Ratner.

DICK. He took it with him. What'll we do?

FLORA. (*Rises and crosses to them*.) Here's a little wedding present for you. (*Takes the deed from the bosom of her dress and hands it to* DICK.) Never underestimate the power of a woman when she's called "Fingers."

DICK. (*Hugs* FLORA.) Aunt Flora, I'm glad you never went to Malaya.

JESS. So am I.

DICK. Come on, Jessica, we're putting out the first extra *The Clarion* has ever published. (*They rush out the front door.*)

FREDERICK. (*As* FLORA *sits on the sofa with* EMILY.) I can't believe it. My little niece getting married.

EMILY. My uncle felt that way about me the first ten or twelve times.

JASON. Mr. Ruggles, I never thought I'd be so glad to see you.

FLORA. Aren't you proud of your little chicks? You're the Honorary President of Charities Anonymous, you know.

FREDERICK. (*Moves Center.*) If that's so, then perhaps you can help me out a little.

PHILIP. Anything at all.

FREDERICK. I'm Chairman of the Policeman's Ball this year and the ticket sales have been going very poorly.

FLORA. What an opportunity. A charity ball.

JASON. Splendid.

FLORA. (*Rises.*) Meeting of Charities Anonymous called to order. All in favor of selling tickets to the Policeman's Ball by whatever means we can— (*She has gestured them to rise and they now stand with their right hands raised.* FREDERICK *coughs and clears his throat. He moves to the windows with his back to them.*) By whatever *honest* means we can, so signify. (*They all take their left hands and cross the third finger of their right hands over the index finger with the left hand.*)

ALL. (*As they smile innocently—all facing front.*) Aye!

The CURTAIN falls

PROPERTY PLOT

ACT ONE

On Stage:
  Cigarettes in pocket (DICK)
Up Center (outside):
  2 suitcases, hatbox, purse containing pill box of saccharin, handkerchief (EMILY)
  Suitcase, briefcase containing written document (PHILIP)
  Suitcase and garment bag (JASON)
Up Center Left (upstairs):
  Sewing bag containing needlepoint, thread, needle and instruction book (FLORA)
Down Left (kitchen):
  Mason jar containing chicken broth (FLORA)
  Tea kettle (FLORA)
  Tea caddy or tea bag (FLORA)
  Tray with four cups, saucers, spoons, creamer, sugar, and lemon (FLORA)
  Teapot covered with tea cozy (FLORA)
  Plate of vanilla and chocolate cookies (FLORA)

ACT TWO

On Stage:
  Sewing bag, etc., on rocking chair (FLORA)
  Briefcase by table Center. 2 pistols, one loaded with blanks inside envelopes, checkbook, pen, stamp, envelope on table (PHILIP)
  Movie magazine on sofa (EMILY)
  Half played-out solitaire on table Left (JASON)
  Playing card, two, stuck up sleeve (JASON)

ACT THREE

Up Center Left (upstairs):
  Black handkerchief (EMILY)
  White handkerchief edged in black (PHILIP)
  Onion (EMILY)
  Handwritten document (PHILIP)
On Stage:
  Sewing bag preset by rocking chair
  Magazine table Left
Up Center (outside):
  Property deed (RATNER)
  Handwritten or typed document (RATNER)

COSTUME PLOT

FLORA

Act One: Summer cotton dress, out of style but originally expensive.
Act Two: Cotton two-piece dress that is a little dressier than previous outfit. Changes to long nightgown, bathrobe and slippers.
Act Three: Summer cotton dress.

JASON

Act One: Dark suit, vest, reverse collar and black dickey attached to collar.
Act Two: Same
Change to long flannel nightgown, nightcap, slippers, robe.
Act Three: Black suit, reverse collar.

EMILY

Act One: Traveling dress, fur jacket, hat, purse, gloves.
Act Two: Quite dressy after-dinner outfit with good jewelry.
Change to nightgown, negligee and slumber-helmet to cover curlers, slippers.
Act Three: A black dress, black handkerchief, black veil covering face, black stockings and shoes.

PHILIP

Act One: Light Summer suit, topcoat.
Act Two: Dark suit.
Act Three: Black suit, black tie, black-edged handkerchief.

RICHARD

Act One: Slacks, sport shirt, jacket.
Act Two: Suit.
Act Three: Slacks, shirt, sweater.

JESSICA

Act One: Good summer cotton dress, obviouly well chosen and rather expensive.
Act Two: Slightly dressier than previous costume and more colorful than the older folks'.
Act Three: Skirt and blouse, cotton and pastel in color.

COSTUME PLOT

HUBERT RATNER

Act One: Sport coat and slacks, shirt and tie.
Act Two: Same.
Act Three: Dark suit.

WARREN COATES

Act One: Loud sport coat, slacks, and tie.
Act Three: White pants, summer sport coat brightly colored.

FREDERICK

Act Three: Dark summer suit, tie in good taste.

SYLVIA

Act Three: Good summer dress or suit, fur neckpiece, fussy hat giving an overall appearance that she spent a lot of time dressing.

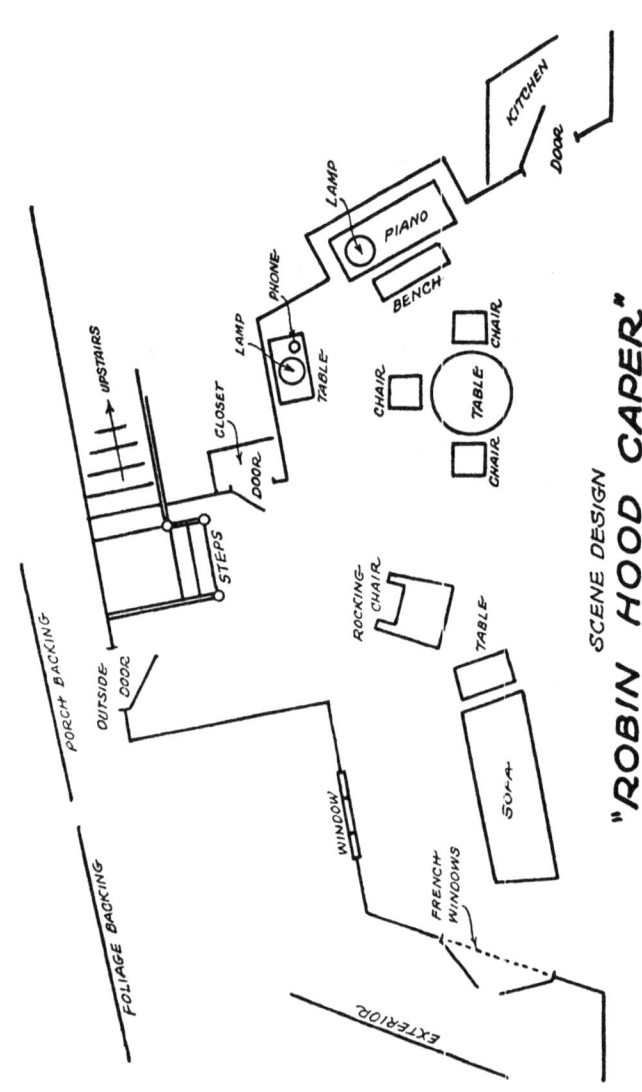

Also By

Fred Carmichael

ALL THE BETTER TO KILL YOU WITH
ANY NUMBER CAN DIE
THE BEST LAID PLANS
DON'T STEP ON MY FOOTPRINT
DONE TO DEATH
DOUBLE IN DIAMONDS
DREAM WORLD
EXIT THE BODY
EXIT WHO?
GUESS WHO'S COMING TO LUNCH
HE'S HAVING A BABY
HEY, NAKED LADY
HOME FREE
HOT PROPERTY
INSIDE LESTER
LAST OF THE CLASS
LUXURY CRUISE
MIXED DOUBLES
MORE THAN MEETS THE EYE
MURDER ON THE RERUN
THE NIGHT IS MY ENEMY
P IS FOR PERFECT
THE PEN IS DEADLIER
PETEY'S CHOICE
SAID THE SPIDER TO THE SPY
SO NICE TO SEE YOU
SURPRISE!
TEN NIGHTS IN A BAR-ROOM
THE THREE MILLION DOLLAR LUNCH
VICTORIA'S HOUSE
WHATEVER HAPPENED TO MRS. KONG?
WHO NEEDS A WALTZ?

SAMUELFRENCH.COM

SKIN DEEP
Jon Lonoff

Comedy / 2m, 2f / Interior Unit Set

In *Skin Deep*, a large, lovable, lonely-heart, named Maureen Mulligan, gives romance one last shot on a blind-date with sweet awkward Joseph Spinelli; she's learned to pepper her speech with jokes to hide insecurities about her weight and appearance, while he's almost dangerously forthright, saying everything that comes to his mind. They both know they're perfect for each other, and in time they come to admit it.

They were set up on the date by Maureen's sister Sheila and her husband Squire, who are having problems of their own: Sheila undergoes a non-stop series of cosmetic surgeries to hang onto the attractive and much-desired Squire, who may or may not have long ago held designs on Maureen, who introduced him to Sheila. With Maureen particularly vulnerable to both hurting and being hurt, the time is ripe for all these unspoken issues to bubble to the surface.

"Warm-hearted comedy ... the laughter was literally show-stopping. A winning play, with enough good-humored laughs and sentiment to keep you smiling from beginning to end."
– *TalkinBroadway.com*

"It's a little Paddy Chayefsky, a lot Neil Simon and a quick-witted, intelligent voyage into the not-so-tranquil seas of middle-aged love and dating. The dialogue is crackling and hilarious; the plot simple but well-turned; the characters endearing and quirky; and lurking beneath the merriment is so much heartache that you'll stand up and cheer when the unlikely couple makes it to the inevitable final clinch."
– *NYTheatreWorld.Com*

SAMUELFRENCH.COM

COCKEYED
William Missouri Downs

Comedy / 3m, 1f / Unit Set
Phil, an average nice guy, is madly in love with the beautiful Sophia. The only problem is that she's unaware of his existence. He tries to introduce himself but she looks right through him. When Phil discovers Sophia has a glass eye, he thinks that might be the problem, but soon realizes that she really can't see him. Perhaps he is caught in a philosophical hyperspace or dualistic reality or perhaps beautiful women are just unaware of nice guys. Armed only with a B.A. in philosophy, Phil sets out to prove his existence and win Sophia's heart. This fast moving farce is the winner of the HotCity Theatre's GreenHouse New Play Festival. The St. Louis Post-Dispatch called Cockeyed a clever romantic comedy, Talkin' Broadway called it "hilarious," while Playback Magazine said that it was "fresh and invigorating."

Winner!
of the HotCity Theatre GreenHouse New Play Festival

"Rocking with laughter...hilarious...polished and engaging work draws heavily on the age-old conventions of farce: improbable situations, exaggerated characters, amazing coincidences, absurd misunderstandings, people hiding in closets and barely missing each other as they run in and out of doors...full of comic momentum as Cockeyed hurtles toward its conclusion."
– Talkin' Broadway

THE OFFICE PLAYS
Two full length plays by Adam Bock

THE RECEPTIONIST
Comedy / 2m, 2f / Interior

At the start of a typical day in the Northeast Office, Beverly deals effortlessly with ringing phones and her colleague's romantic troubles. But the appearance of a charming rep from the Central Office disrupts the friendly routine. And as the true nature of the company's business becomes apparent, The Receptionist raises disquieting, provocative questions about the consequences of complicity with evil.

"...Mr. Bock's poisoned Post-it note of a play."
– *New York Times*

"Bock's intense initial focus on the routine goes to the heart of *The Receptionist's* pointed, painfully timely allegory... elliptical, provocative play..."
– *Time Out New York*

THE THUGS
Comedy / 2m, 6f / Interior

The Obie Award winning dark comedy about work, thunder and the mysterious things that are happening on the 9th floor of a big law firm. When a group of temps try to discover the secrets that lurk in the hidden crevices of their workplace, they realize they would rather believe in gossip and rumors than face dangerous realities.

"Bock starts you off giggling, but leaves you with a chill."
– *Time Out New York*

"... a delightfully paranoid little nightmare that is both more chillingly realistic and pointedly absurd than anything John Grisham ever dreamed up."
– *New York Times*

SAMUELFRENCH.COM

TREASURE ISLAND
Ken Ludwig

All Groups / Adventure / 10m, 1f (doubling) / Areas
Based on the masterful adventure novel by Robert Louis Stevenson, *Treasure Island* is a stunning yarn of piracy on the tropical seas. It begins at an inn on the Devon coast of England in 1775 and quickly becomes an unforgettable tale of treachery and mayhem featuring a host of legendary swashbucklers including the dangerous Billy Bones (played unforgettably in the movies by Lionel Barrymore), the sinister two-timing Israel Hands, the brassy woman pirate Anne Bonney, and the hideous form of evil incarnate, Blind Pew. At the center of it all are Jim Hawkins, a 14-year-old boy who longs for adventure, and the infamous Long John Silver, who is a complex study of good and evil, perhaps the most famous hero-villain of all time. Silver is an unscrupulous buccaneer-rogue whose greedy quest for gold, coupled with his affection for Jim, cannot help but win the heart of every soul who has ever longed for romance, treasure and adventure.

www.ingramcontent.com/pod-product-compliance
Lightning Source LLC
Chambersburg PA
CBHW070646300426
44111CB00013B/2298